ELK
STOPPED PLAY

ELK
STOPPED PLAY

AND OTHER TALES FROM *WISDEN*'S
'CRICKET ROUND THE WORLD'

EDITED BY

Charlie Connelly

WITH A FOREWORD BY

Michael Palin

B L O O M S B U R Y

LONDON · NEW DELHI · NEW YORK · SYDNEY

First published in Great Britain 2014

Original material
Copyright © Charlie Connelly 2014

Material reproduced from
Wisden Cricketers' Almanack
© John Wisden & Co

Foreword copyright © 2014 Michael Palin

Illustrated letters copyright © David Bromley 2014

The moral right of the author has been asserted

No part of this book may be used or reproduced in any manner
whatsoever without written permission from the publisher except in the
case of brief quotations embedded in critical articles or reviews

Every reasonable effort has been made to trace copyright holders of
material reproduced in this book, but if any have been inadvertently
overlooked the publishers would be glad to hear from them.

John Wisden and Co

An imprint of Bloomsbury Publishing plc
50 Bedford Square
London
WC1B 3DP

www.wisden.com

Bloomsbury Publishing, London, New Delhi, New York and Sydney

A CIP catalogue record for this book is available from the British Library

ISBN 978 1 4088 3237 0

10 9 8 7 6 5 4 3 2 1

Typeset by Saxon Graphics Ltd, Derby
Printed and bound in Great Britain by CPI Group (UK) Ltd,
Croydon CR0 4YY

To my dad, George Connelly, for teaching me from an early age the soul-enriching benefits of both cricket and travel.

ACKNOWLEDGEMENTS

I'd like to thank Scyld Berry for his support for and encouragement of the initial idea, and Christopher Lane and Charlotte Atyeo for all their faith, help and patience in its execution. Thanks to Matthew Engel who established the section in the first place, to Lawrence Booth, Graeme Wright, Hugh Chevallier, Tony Munro, Timothy Abraham and James Coyne – past and current editors of Cricket Round the World – and also to Mahendra Mapagunaratne, for his consistent help with the Cricket Round the World section. Finally, all my love and thanks to Jude for being the finest and most supportive cricket widow the global game has ever seen.

"The game is essentially English, and though our countrymen carry it abroad wherever they go, it is difficult to inoculate or knock it into the foreigner. The Italians are too fat for cricket, the French too thin, the Dutch too dumpy, the Belgians too bilious, the Flemish too flatulent, the East Indians too peppery, the Laplanders too bow-legged, the Swiss too sentimental, the Greeks too lazy, the Egyptians too long in the neck, and the Germans too short in the wind."

Charles Box, *The Theory and Practice of Cricket*, 1868

FOREWORD

We tend to think of cricket as the quintessential English game, associated with tall trees, church towers, snug pubs and overgrown outfields, but in my travels I've seen it played in very different surroundings. Halfway up a mountain in Pakistan, where a lofted six could send the ball ten thousand feet into the Indus valley and where a boundary catch could be fatal; on the deck of a container ship; in car parks; on railway lines; and once, on my *Full Circle* journey, on a brownfield site in Hanoi belonging to the Vietnamese Air Force. This had many problems, one being the non-appearance of the captain who was bringing the pitch. When eventually he arrived, carrying twenty-two yards of coconut matting over his shoulder, a head bearing the cap and red star of the People's Army popped up from behind a wall, and watched with increasing bewilderment as the two teams, India and the Rest of the World, limbered up. When the first boundary was struck hard towards the wall, the head disappeared smartly. Midway through the third over, a phone rang in the captain's pocket as he crouched at third slip. Did we know that this was a sensitive military area? The captain vainly tried to explain that it was just a game, when an entire detachment of soldiers, the majority of them women, marched out to bring the game to a premature close of play.

Anything that the military see as a threat has to have something going for it, and if I were a paranoid general I would be extremely concerned about the revelations in Charlie Connelly's book. It's clear that cricket, with all its attendant subversive potential, is creeping across the world. From Antarctica to Ethiopia, from North Korea to St Helena, there are fielders fanning out and guards being taken. Balls have been struck across national boundaries and doubtless from one hemisphere to another. I know this and Charlie Connelly knows this because the indispensable oracle that is *Wisden Cricketers' Almanack* has been charting every detail of cricket's global advance. This is how we know that a hundred years ago there was a King of Tonga who inflicted so much cricket on his subjects that they had to limit the days it was played, "to avert famine". Thanks to *Wisden* and Connelly I now know that Don Bradman's grandmother was Italian, that there is an Estonian Cricket Board, and that one of the greatest of all team names, the Gondwanaland Occasionals, harks back to a time before the continents assumed their present shape, when cricket was played by the very earliest life forms. This book is brimful of the sort of esoteric facts that cricket followers love, but it's also a terrific travel book, to be read not just with a Wisden by your side, but an atlas too. And, of course, a large gin and tonic. Or a caipirinha, a sliwowitz or a stiff pisco sour.

Elk Stopped Play is a universal pleasure and a hugely enjoyable reminder of a game which combines unquenchable enthusiasm with incomparable eccentricity. And it's good to know that there is barely a corner of God's earth where you can walk without at least some chance of being hit by a cricket ball.

Michael Palin
London, July 2013

INTRODUCTION

When I was a boy my sister and I were sent over to The Hague one summer to stay with some Dutch friends of our parents. I wasn't happy. At Headingley New Zealand were on their way to their first-ever Test victory in England, and I'd become a little bit obsessed with Lance Cairns; he of the shoulderless club of a bat with which he'd smite enormous sixes to all corners, before lumbering up to the wicket with the grace and elegance of a prop forward learning to unicycle, and bowl out teams with his chest-on, banana-shaped outswingers.

But just as Cairns was celebrating taking seven English wickets on the first day as part of a performance that would earn him the Man of the Match award, I was being plucked from the sofa and the company of Jim Laker and Peter West and deposited on an aeroplane to Holland where, as far as I knew, they'd never even *heard* of cricket.

Fascinating city though The Hague undoubtedly is, in hindsight I can't help thinking my hosts must have noticed how underwhelmed I was by the Gemeentemuseum and the Madurodam miniature park. The medieval town centre would ordinarily have coaxed forth wide-eyed wonder, or at least polite "oohs" and "ahhs", but instead I was scanning the shop fronts in vain for signs of an English newspaper that might bring news from Headingley. It was summer, there was a Test match on, my new favourite player was taking it by storm, and here I was in a barren cricketing wasteland that might as well have been on the other side of the Horsehead Nebula as the North Sea. I'd never been wrenched from cricket like this before and at just 12 years old I was already finding life outside its comforting linseed-infused cocoon to be riddled with crushing ennui.

One afternoon, we were in the back of the car on our way somewhere and I was wondering wistfully what damage Lance's batting might have caused windows within a half-mile radius of the Kirkstall Lane end when, between some trees, I saw what I assumed at first to be a mirage induced by my cricket cold turkey. The car slowed in traffic as we got closer, and my mouth fell open as I realised what I was seeing.

There was a cricket match going on. A proper one. Everyone was in whites. There were umpires in long white coats. There was a pavilion. There was a scattering of spectators. I wound down the window as the bowler ran up and windmilled his arms. The batsman got on to the front foot, swung, and half a second later I heard that familiar satisfying "pock" of sweet spot on leather. The fielder at cover turned disconsolately and jogged after the ball as a ripple of applause drifted across to me through the trees. Then the traffic moved again, the match disappeared behind us, and we carried on to wherever we were going as if nothing had happened.

It had either been a delicious illusion or I'd just seen a cricket match. In Holland. And it looked just like real cricket. *Proper* cricket, with the clatter of tin numbers as someone updated the scoreboard that stood propped against a table, floppy sunhats, bored girlfriends in deckchairs reading magazines, the billows of dust as a batsman thumped his guard into the crease, scorers acknowledging the umpires' signals, a boy throwing down balls to the next batsman on the boundary, players padded up and sitting on benches in that legs-wide-apart pose that all impending batsmen adopt everywhere. It looked, to all intents and purposes, just like the real thing.

Of course, it *was* the real thing. Indeed, cricket has been played in the Netherlands since British soldiers introduced it during the Napoleonic Wars. I didn't know it at the time but as I was staring open-mouthed at the flannelled mirages before me, it was exactly 100 years since the foundation of the Dutch game's governing body in 1883, and the first match played by a Dutch national team had taken place right there in The Hague in 1881 against Uxbridge CC – quite possibly, for all I know, on the very same ground I'd passed that day.

I know all this now because I've just looked it up on the internet. In 1983 however, there was no internet. Also, in 1983 there was no "Cricket Round the World" section in *Wisden*, so as far as I was concerned the world cricket map consisted of nothing more than the Test-playing nations and a vast blank expanse marked "here be dragons". To find a real cricket match in, of all places, downtown Den Haag, well, I was astonished to say the least. I'm fairly sure I didn't even think about Lance Cairns for a good ten minutes.

Today Dutch cricket is more familiar to us. We've seen their team at the World Cup, and I'm sure most of us could even spell Ryan ten Doeschate correctly first time if we really put our minds to it. Back then, however, cricket outside the Test arena was to me no more than a rumour, the stuff of sea monsters and mermaids. When Derbyshire signed the rangy Danish pace bowler Ole Mortensen in 1983, for example, he seemed to me to be some kind of freak of nature – how on earth could a professional cricketer come from *Denmark*? Combined with his foppish fringe and Douglas Fairbanks moustache, even his first name seemed to lend him an air of swaggering mystery (that is until I found out it wasn't pronounced "*oh-LAY*" after all, but the rather less flamboyant "*Ull*"). I followed his career closely, completely astounded by his sheer Danishness. Clearly, when you're finding a former tax inspector from Copenhagen awe-strikingly enigmatic, your cricket horizons are in need of expansion, and fast.

These strange cricketing foreigners weren't just emerging from Holland and Denmark, either. As we will see in these pages, cricket was and is happening all over the world and in some pretty unlikely locations too. In 1993 the Almanack's new editor Matthew Engel had the foresight and vision to introduce the Cricket Round the World section in order to reflect the game's more global aspects.

There were just nine nations featured that first year, ranging in exoticism from Nepal to Belgium (Denmark and the Netherlands already had sections to themselves), but in two decades Cricket Round the World has grown and developed into such an iron horse of the Almanack that it feels as if it's always been there. More than 140 nations or territories have now been featured, with new ones appearing every year – in the 2013 *Wisden* alone seven new entries appeared.

Wisden had sometimes made the occasional foray into the world beyond the traditional Test-playing nations before the advent of Cricket Round the World – as with Denmark and the Netherlands. The 1965 *Wisden*, for example, reported on the former Australia wicketkeeper Bert Oldfield's month in Ethiopia attempting to introduce cricket into schools. "Perhaps the day may not be far distant when Ethiopia will be challenging England and Australia to Test matches," suggests the piece with tongue wedged firmly in cheek. But perhaps the most intriguing aspect of Oldfield's trip was his twenty-minute audience with the Ethiopian emperor Haile Selassie, during which the Lion of Judah was presented with a cricket bat as a gift from the Australian prime minister Sir Robert Menzies. I, for one, would love to have been a fly on the wall for *that* particular conversation.

Fiji featured in 1974 and Nepal in 1992, but probably my favourite pre-Cricket Round the World item is the obituary of George Tubow II, King of Tonga, who was eulogised in the 1919 Almanack.

"The last of the independent kings in the Pacific," lamented the tribute. "Died April, aged 46. Very fond of cricket, gaining his love of the game while at school in Auckland. His subjects became so devoted to the game that it was necessary to prohibit it on six days of the week to avert famine, the plantations being entirely neglected for the cricket field."

It may have pre-dated Cricket Round the World by more than 70 years but all the ingredients are there: the exotic location, a larger-than-life character, the idiosyncratic place of cricket in an unexpected land and the carefully underplayed "wow" moment as a pay-off; in this case how people were so engrossed in playing cricket that it nearly led to a national famine. Obituary it may have been, but that short item among the vast litany of First World War dead remains the template and archetype for the classic Cricket Round the World entry.

It's a template that works too, and is growing and developing every year. Whenever a new *Wisden* appears, Cricket Round the World is the section I head for first. Before the Five Cricketers of the Year, before the Notes by the Editor – they all come behind finding out which global backwaters have sent in their couple of paragraphs. I often picture a correspondent in a snowbound tin shed, typing his copy while wrapped in furs, or despatching it with an errand boy to the telegraph station as a distant ukulele trills, before returning to the bar, patting the pockets of his sweat-stained safari suit for his pipe and matches, and ordering another banana daiquiri.

With each passing year there's another spellbinding collection of tales detailing quirky circumstances and against-the-odds achievements that can only inspire cricketers and non-cricketers alike. If anyone ever asks me what makes the game of cricket special, I point them towards this section of the Almanack: there are few parts of *Wisden*, or indeed any cricket publication, that can eclipse the sheer variety and spirit contained in those pages. From ICC Associate Members with a half-decent chance of reaching the World Cup (organisational chicanery notwithstanding) to remote global outposts with dustbins for stumps and ingenious local rules to accommodate quirks in the prevailing conditions, all cricketing life is there. In the turn of a page you can be transported from frostbitten fingers on frozen tundra to sweltering jungle clearings or dusty rock-strewn expanses under relentless hot sun. And at the centre of it all, of course, there's always cricket. Most of all though, Cricket Round the World celebrates two aspects of the game largely responsible for its continued existence and success: aspiration and fun.

There's the aspiration of the stronger nations as they strive to improve themselves and challenge the established order; nations like Argentina and Denmark, blessed with fine players and long-embedded organisational structures designed to optimise their potential as far as possible despite the competing attractions of football and other more established sports.

There are also the nations and territories for whom dreams of playing at the World Cup are left behind on the pillow when waking every morning; places where cricket is played for recreation and enjoyment: the outcrops like St Helena and Niue Island; out-of-the-way places that tend to be where cricket once arrived with the military and the missionary, the game as a legacy of cultural and historical imprints that remain in the eternal struggle between bat and ball. There are examples of cricket in adversity, such as the stories found in the squalid surroundings of refugee holding camps on Nauru and Christmas Island, for example, and cricket being played among soldiers in Iraq even to the point of an "Ashes in the Desert" being contested between British and Australian troops. And of course there are the quirky knock-ups in places with no historical connection to the game; reports of matches played for the sheer devilment, literally from pole to pole, born out of a love of cricket combined with a determined eccentricity whose levels are surely unmatched in any other sport. This whole range of stories is unfailingly underpinned by an overriding and unquenchable love of the game itself.

One could argue – and in fact I *would* argue – that it's in places like these that the ill-defined and much sought-after spirit of cricket shines brightest. It takes a level of commitment to play cricket that other popular sports don't require: anyone can play football, you just need a ball of some kind and space of just about any dimensions. But while cricket utilises one of the oldest and most basic tenets of human sporting activity – hitting a ball with a stick – it does need equipment, however basic or improvised it may turn out to be. The game also needs a certain amount of flat terrain, a degree of technique and a passing knowledge of at least the basic laws before play can begin in earnest.

It takes a special kind of determination to stage a game of cricket on, say, a tiny, far-flung island, or in a country with no cricketing history where the game is met by locals with looks of bafflement, bewilderment, suspicion or even fear. The hardy souls who achieve these things – be they nostalgic expats, tourists or curiosity-piqued locals – are well worth their place in the Almanack alongside the greats of the past and present.

The existence of Cricket Round the World also reflects the global events, cultural developments and even patterns of migration of the last 20 years and beyond. Indian, Sri Lankan and Pakistani migrant workers and students are currently the most active and enthusiastic cricket evangelists, kick-starting the game in places as diverse as the former Soviet Union and tiny Pacific islands. Some of the countries featured here are younger than *Wisden* itself, while the presence within its pages of nations like Austria and Kazakhstan shows how the game is spreading way beyond the faded tenets of empire – and spreading faster than ever before.

Television has taken cricket into the unlikeliest of living-rooms, prompting complete novices from Iceland to Bhutan to take up the game. The internet has made the acquiring of information, inspiration and equipment more straightforward than ever before, meaning a game previously regarded in some quarters as one of empire is now a truly and undeniably global phenomenon.

Entries such as those featuring matches played by soldiers in Iraq and in the refugee detention centres also illustrate the role of cricket in preserving a sense of civilisation and normality in the most hellish and testing of circumstances. What could be further from the violence and bloodshed of war on the doorstep, or the fear and anxiety of detention in a refugee camp than the calm, reassuring rhythms of a game of cricket? In strange places and difficult situations we are always comforted by the familiar: the shared rituals and gentle nuances of a game of cricket are ideally suited to make difficult situations in difficult locations at least a little more bearable, even if it is just for an afternoon. For a Sri Lankan sweltering in roasting hot tents on the lunar landscape of Nauru after a perilous boat journey across the Indian Ocean as he waits for his Australian asylum application to be considered – something that could take many years – having a game of cricket to look forward to might just be the one thing that can keep him going through the relentless and endless slow passing of days.

Poignant human stories like these stud the knockabout fun and straightforward enthusiasms that make up much of the Cricket Round the World section: the emergence of Afghan cricket is an obvious example, and I've often wondered whatever became of the man Prague CC unearthed, as reported in the Czech Republic entry in the 1998 *Wisden*, apparently "a talented Pakistani batsman; unfortunately he was in a refugee camp and is believed to have been deported".

In every Cricket Round the World entry, from whichever nation or territory it might have come, whether the game is being played in trying circumstances or just passing an afternoon among a group of friends, there are always the common cricket themes of hope, fair play, achievement, aspiration and fun, shared across borders, oceans and continents, far away from the hype of the IPL and the endless treadmill of Test and one-day international cricket. This is why I strongly believe that the heart of cricket can be found beating in those few pages each year.

What can also be found in the Cricket Round the World section is some extremely good travel writing. These nuggets of prose from places many of us would be hard-pressed to point to on a map provide some eloquent, valuable and evocative portraits of life in places we'll never see. Viewed through the prism of the game we love, the collected Cricket Round the World entries of the last 20 years or so provide a fascinating portrait of human life all over the planet, and these portraits are usually couched in some very fine writing indeed. As a travel writer myself, I have to read some pretty awful travel prose – all "cities of contrasts" and "colourful markets" – most of which never comes close to capturing the real spirit and essence of a place. *Wisden* eschews the flowery and the clichéd in favour of understated prose that tells a cricket story while adding a remarkable amount of local colour. Canon Nicholas Turner's entry about cricket on Ascension Island that appeared in the 1996 *Wisden*, for example, told me in a few sentences more about culture and life on a remote island in the Atlantic Ocean than just about everything else written on the subject put together.

Elk Stopped Play revisits, contextualises and expands upon the amazing accounts that have appeared in the pages of *Wisden* over the last two decades. Each year Cricket Round the World bursts with wonderful achievements, outstanding performances, laugh-out-loud anecdotes and frequently poignant human stories, often against considerable odds. I've tried to reflect all of these in selecting my favourites here. As a travel writer who has always looked for the unusual, and a (bad) cricketer who's always enjoyed playing in unexpected places – I believe I still hold the record for the westernmost cover-drive on the European continent, a satisfying tonk through sheep droppings and boulders at the western tip of Valentia Island off the far south-west of Ireland – I have unashamedly favoured the more niche and quirky locations and stories in this collection. Some of the stories I've chosen speak for themselves and stand alone; in some cases I've fleshed out the detail, added a little more context and brought things up to date, and in others they've been a stepping stone to a wider exploration of that nation's cricket. I hope I've succeeded in my aims of celebrating the diverse and fascinating nature of cricket around the world and of paying tribute to some of the loyal and gifted *Wisden* correspondents scattered across the globe. It's been my pleasure to correspond with some of them in the course of preparing this book and wherever I've tracked them down, however long it's been since their *Wisden* contribution, I've found exactly the same levels of passion, enthusiasm and kindness flourishing wherever in the world they happen to be.

As I write these words the 150th *Wisden Cricketers' Almanack* is upon us. I sincerely hope that John Wisden himself would approve of this selection of stories, just as I'm sure he would enjoy the Almanack's annual tour of global cricket. After all, Wisden – as a member of the 1859 All-England squad that undertook the first-ever overseas cricket tour to America – was a pioneering cricket globetrotter himself. In his wonderful history of the Almanack, *The Little Wonder*, Robert Winder tells of how on the rough Atlantic crossing that sent passengers stumbling and had crockery shattering on the floor, Wisden recorded in his journal that the pitch required "the immediate use of the heavy roller".

With its dry, understated wit inspired by a desire for the normality of cricket in the face of extreme circumstances, it's a line that could have come straight from the pages of Cricket Round the World itself.

ANGOLA

In Angola, a country devastated by civil war since gaining
independence from Portugal in 1975, cricket has formed a bond
between the Indian and Pakistani communities. Kashmir and other
issues are forgotten as around 20 hardy souls meet three times a
week to play next to a floodlit football ground in the capital Luanda.
It's a taste of home life, apparently instigated when two Indians
began playing with a piece of wood and two tennis balls in 1994.
Narinder Pal Singh, **Wisden 2003**

ANTARCTICA

The packed slip cordon at the annual Casey Base cricket match has
little to do with swing, seam or – with temperatures hovering
around freezing – conserving body heat. It's more a question of
knowing that a missed catch will condemn the guilty fielder to a trek
down treacherous icy slopes to fetch the ball from a small meltwater
lake. The fixture is traditionally played each Casey Day (February
12), the anniversary of the founding of the Australian Antarctic
Research Station, some 3,880 km south of Perth and 2,580 km
from the South Pole. Teams comprise Australian scientists and
visitors of varying nationalities. The pitch is a cement helipad,

ensuring generous bounce. Naturally, local rules apply: should the tennis ball – this isn't the place to break the triple-glazed windows – ricochet off the Red Shed, the two-storey living quarters, it's four; over the roof is six; hitting the station leader at the barbecue is instant dismissal, which still somehow proves an irresistible target. Post-match analysis is often fuelled by ample quantities of Antarctica's own home brew, known as Penguin's Piss. *John Rich*, **Wisden 2003**

The continent of Antarctica has hosted more cricket matches than you might think, not all of them lubricated by Penguin Piss either (which, all things considered, is probably for the best). Cricket remains part of the annual February celebrations at Casey Station, situated in the Australian Antarctic Territory overlooking the northern side of the Bailey Peninsula (its rugged, imposing nature suggesting it may have been named after Trevor rather than the Australian politician Richard). February is one of the more amenable months to cricket temperature-wise, settling between a balmy -5°C and a sweltering -1°C. In July and August, when most of us this side of the equator are dozing in the sun – waking only when a team-mate reminds us we're bowling and there are still three deliveries left in the over – the Casey cricketers see the mercury plummet to a parky -37°C. It's not just the weather that makes cricket in the Antarctic taxing either, there's the local wildlife to contend with too. An Australia Day game at the base was once interrupted when an elephant seal lolloped on to the pitch and made its intentions to remain parked on a good length for some time stubbornly clear.

But while the seal-whispering cricketing scientists at Casey are the continent's "home" team – and probably the closest Antarctica will ever get to a national side – a number of others have braved the ice and tundra with bat and ball. Harry Thompson's experiences detailed in his book *Penguins Stopped Play* set the bar high for South Pole cricket even though the impromptu circumstances –

there was only an oar available for use as a bat, for example – meant that it was never destined to be a textbook display of the cricketing arts. But others were coming. And others had been.

Antarctica's first instance of a follow-on was arguably Captain Scott's doomed polar expedition of 1912 in which he was always well behind Roald Amundsen with little or no hope of saving the game. Exactly 100 years later another English explorer arrived in Antarctica determined to avenge Scott's defeat by the Norwegian at least on the cricket field. Neil Laughton, a former Royal Marine commando and ex-member of the SAS, led three men on a Scott centenary memorial expedition to the South Pole during the winter of 2011–12. Among the equipment they hauled on foot for the last 100 miles were a plastic cricket bat and a high-visibility orange ball, with which they intended to mark the centenary of Scott's arrival at the Pole by staging a cricket match against the scientists at the Amundsen–Scott research centre at the Geographical South Pole. The pitch was cleared with a snowmobile, blizzards held off and the game was able to commence on January 17, 2012, 100 years to the day after Scott's arrival at the Pole. The game, incidentally, was given added cricketing gravitas by the presence as umpire of former Wisden editor Matthew Engel.

Laughton explained that he'd chosen cricket because it was "an iconic British sport and a team game". Whether it felt like an iconic sport to the players as the wind chill took the temperature down into the minus thirties and, at 10,000ft above sea level, the altitude made even nabbing a single a lung-busting challenge, we'll probably never know. Either way Laughton's British team beat a team dubbed The Rest of the World but largely comprising Australian trekkers who'd reached the Pole via a different route, by two wickets. There was no boundary so every run scored was actually run: this is challenging enough in any circumstances but particularly when you're clad from head to toe in polar survival gear and the air isn't exactly bursting with oxygen. The quality of the cricket was compromised further when the plastic bat snapped in half due to the freezing temperatures and the game had to be completed with its shattered remains. This was a game that could never be described as "one for the purists", but then it was probably never intended as such.

Laughton was happy with the result though, not least because he felt it might offer Scott himself a crumb of comfort 100 years after Amundsen had beaten him to the punch. "With the British outcome, at least he is hopefully looking down on us and this has put a smile on his face," he said. It was an appropriate result for other reasons too: exactly a century before on January 17, 1912, as Scott arrived at the pole to find Amundsen's Norwegian flag planted proprietarily in the snow, J. W. H. T. Douglas's England had also beaten Australia, by seven wickets at Adelaide, to take a 2–1 lead in the Ashes, thanks largely to Jack Hobbs's 187 in the first innings.

I've tried in vain to find a cricket connection to Scott himself. It seems that, while he carried some fairly idiosyncratic items south with him – a full china dinner service, the complete works of Thomas Hardy and an upright piano, for example – a cricket bat was not among them.

Incidentally, although this was Antarctica's first appearance in Cricket Round the World, it wasn't the continent's first mention in the Almanack. The 1986 *Wisden* featured a paragraph tucked away at the bottom of the "Scottish Cricket in 1985" entry. Anticipating in both tone and subject matter the dedicated section that was still seven years away, the item read:

"What was almost certainly the most southerly game of cricket ever played, and the coldest, took place in Antarctica, 700 kilometres from the South Pole, on January 11, 1985, between two teams drawn from the 60 scientists, lawyers, environmentalists and administrators engaged in an international workshop being held at the Beardmore South Camp and concerned with the Antarctic Treaty. New Zealand's representative on the Treaty, Christopher Beeby, captained the Gondwanaland Occasionals with players from

Australia, New Zealand and South Africa. A British delegate to the conference, Arthur Watts, captained the Beardmore Casuals, a basically British team. The stumps were improvised, the pitch, such as it was, had been rolled by a Hercules transport aircraft, and the 'midnight sun' allowed play to continue until 11pm. The Occasionals (129) beat the Casuals (102) by 27 runs."

One can't help thinking that while "Occasionals" might be an appropriate name for an Antarctic cricket team, calling any side that's made it to the very bottom of the world determined to have a game of cricket "Casuals" is a little unfair.

The match was organised by the Casuals' skipper Sir Arthur Watts, who in his youth had played Minor Counties cricket for Shropshire, and took place on the Bowden Nevé at a latitude of roughly 84 degrees south. The wicket was a board with painted stumps, and the bails were two beer-cans whose contents froze immediately. The Casuals' 102 featured a top score of 22 by Greenpeace's Roger Wilson, while the Occasionals' leading scorer was Trevor Hatheron, a scientist from New Zealand, who made a nifty 24. While these individual scores might not look all that impressive on paper, they are possibly put into context by the fact that no less than 13 batsmen in the match were recorded as "retired frozen".

However, even this wasn't the first game of cricket at the South Pole. Cricket's Antarctic debut is believed to date back as far as 1969, when a match took place using the South Pole itself – a red-and-white striped shaft like a giant barber's pole – as a wicket. The game featured the former New Zealand captain John Reid – the first man to lead them to Test match wins at home and away – but was a short-lived affair: a meaty biff by the New Zealander disappeared into a snowdrift and the proceedings had to be abandoned.

Sir Arthur Watts reacted haughtily when it was put to him that his game hadn't been the first at the South Pole as he'd claimed. Reid's knockabout with three colleagues was not, he protested, a proper match.

"This deplorable attempt to deprive our game of its status as a 'first' wholly ignores the difference between a four-man frolic and an organised match played between two full teams," he huffed. "And, of course, we did not use a real cricket ball, since we foresaw what would happen if we did: a lost ball buried deep in the snow, as the four-man frolic quickly discovered."

A notable feature of Reid's "four-man frolic" was that, with the wicket being the South Pole itself, every shot played travelled north.

Given the necessary allowances made to the laws in such extreme circumstances one hopes that at least one player at the South Pole took the opportunity to hit the ball and then run around the wicket. It would be quite something to say that you'd scored a single by running around the world.

ASCENSION ISLAND

Plans are afoot to return cricket to one of the world's most distinctive grounds. The barren, volcanic rock of Ascension Island in the South Atlantic is believed to be the only place where "wedding stopped play" – to be resumed 40 minutes later as the last of the congregation left for the reception. The little Church of St Mary the Virgin is inside the boundary and, when it was restored in 1993, with a new slate roof, cricket moved to a new and larger ground at the island's RAF camp, where floodlit play is possible. However, the move has not been popular with the crowds (all things are relative – the total population is only 1,200) and Dr Sukhtanker, the resident surgeon and cricketing supremo, intends to take the game back to its original venue. Cricket on Ascension, uninhabited until the Royal Navy landed in 1815, took off when West Indian workers arrived in the mid-1960s to build a relay station. They started league cricket, which has been kept going by South Africans working for the cable company, and the RAF, who returned during the Falklands War.

They have provided teaching input for the workers from St Helena who are employed here. St Helenians have a natural aptitude for the game, and have developed good technique, with two exceptions: the concrete strip offers little chance of spin, and the short boundaries – combined with American influence – have encouraged some towards the high baseball slog. The cricket field by the church, which used to be the army parade ground, is actually rolled volcanic ash, with not a blade of grass in sight, and the outfield is very fast. The ball used is a composite – a leather ball would be torn to shreds – and we need several per game there, to replace those which get stuck on the church roof or among the stores waiting to be loaded onto the next ship. A dusty trade wind always blows across the pitch, but it is what people seem to prefer and it is indeed a fine setting, if you can find some shade: the four sides comprising the small, white church, a smooth, dark red, volcanic cone, the ageing, arcaded barracks, and the dark blue ocean with its giant waves crashing in towards the anchorage below. *Canon Nicholas Turner, Vicar of Ascension* **Wisden 1996**

Stuck right in the middle of the South Atlantic, a thousand miles from Africa and 1,400 miles from South America, Ascension is certainly one of the more remote places ever to have hosted cricket. Indeed it's one of the more remote places ever to have hosted anything at all. Named after the day in 1503 it was discovered by the magnificently named Portuguese explorer Afonso d'Alberquerque (it had actually been discovered two years earlier by a Galician, but it seems he forgot to tell anyone), Ascension possibly saw its first cricket action with the arrival in 1815 of British troops on the island, garrisoned there in order to help keep an eye on Napoleon who had been exiled to St Helena some 800 miles to the south-east. With eyesight *that* good they must have been fair cricketers. The volcanic island's suitability as a venue for cricket may also be detected in the comment of the 19th-century French naturalist René Primevère Lesson, when he said of Ascension that "the English nation alone would have thought of making the island of Ascension a productive spot". If the English can make a home in such unpromising surroundings then cricket surely won't be far behind.

Canon Nicholas Turner's contribution to the 1996 *Wisden* is one of my favourite Cricket Round the World entries. With its strong sense of place, wry humour, local detail and clear love of the game, it showcases everything that's special about cricket in unusual places.

He arrived on the island with his wife in 1991, and they would remain for five years. "I am a priest of the Church of England and my wife Ann is a deacon," he told me from his current home in West Yorkshire. "When we got married we realised we would need to find a new parish and answered the advertisement for Ascension Island, partly because it had been vacant for a long time, and partly because it would give us the opportunity to work out our joint ministry without the interference of English bishops (liberals are so conservative – that's a Church problem). In the end, we loved it and stayed longer than any clergy since the church was built."

Despite playing down his cricketing talents ("I was a wicketkeeper in the school second eleven, but the only cricket I played as an adult was in a San Francisco league: one summer while I was looking after a parish there I discovered a moderate ability as a spin bowler"), Canon Turner was at the heart of Ascension cricket during his entire time there and was the ideal *Wisden* correspondent. Two aspects of his Ascension entry stood out for me: the day a wedding stopped play and the desire of Dr Sukhtanker to return Ascension cricket to its spiritual home. When I asked about the wedding incident, 17 years on he remembers the important things first: "The score was 83 for five," he said, "that has stuck with me for life."

The groom, a young RAF corporal, was only scheduled to be stationed on Ascension for a few months, but saw the posting as an ideal opportunity to circumvent some tricky issues.

"He and his fiancée had been under pressure from their families to do the wedding just so, but instead they came up with the simple idea of having it 4,000 miles away. This made for a simpler, smaller affair, free of interference and with wonderful photos at sunset on the beach. A whitewashed open-top Land Rover stood in for the Rolls-Royce."

The necessity for a nuptial-related cessation of play came about because the church didn't have glass windows, only wooden louvres that let in light, air and, potentially, the boisterous hullabaloo of a keenly contested cricket match right on its doorstep.

"I hadn't realised there was going to be a league fixture that day," said Canon Turner, "but the teams were very good-natured about it and took their enforced break with equanimity.".

While marital and cricketing bliss was mutually assured, alas it appears that Dr Sukhtanker's dream of bringing Ascension cricket home was never realised. And the church was again the catalyst.

"As far as I can tell, the move never happened. The church roof was the main problem. For its 150th anniversary in 1993, the RAF had adopted St Mary's as a garrison church and undertook a comprehensive restoration, which involved constructing a complete new roof. It was this work that forced the closure of the cricket field, because half of it was covered with building supplies and huts. Cricket had to move up to the Travellers playing field, further up the volcano and therefore cooler – Georgetown has always been the hottest part of the island.

"When the work was finished, the old lead roof had been replaced with smart black tiles, and the cricketers were fearful of breaking the new tiles. The old rules were that if you hit the roof it counted as a six, hit the wall and it was a four: the entire church and surrounding wall were inside the running track which formed the boundary so we needed these local adjustments to the laws. In hindsight I suspect my reason for writing that 1996 piece was to add weight to the campaign for a return to the island's historic ground. Perhaps I'd even been urged to do so by 'Shub', as Dr Sukhtanker was affectionately known. I do remember that there was a very large supply of surplus tiles that were carefully stored away, and promises were made that at the end of each season any broken tiles would be replaced. I can clearly remember checking all this out and speaking to team captains and so on, but despite those assurances I don't think we succeeded."

Most of the remote places featured in Cricket Round the World enjoy aspects of the game unique to their location. The local rule concerning the St Mary's church roof is a prime example, albeit one that inadvertently contributed to cricket leaving the ground altogether for fear of ecclesiastical tile-breakage. These out-of-the-way places often face their own unique cricket-related problems and issues, with Ascension being no exception.

"As with every other part of island life, individuals could make a huge difference for a short time, only to leave just when you got used to them," recalled Canon Turner. "Certainly, the RAF brought a fair number of good sportsmen into the pool of players, though the longer serving Saints – as the island-born residents are known – had much greater experience of the conditions. Balls were the big expense, as they deteriorated so rapidly and so many were lost, particularly on the pier-head side among the containers and other portside clutter.

"Even in the 'winter' season, it was always extremely hot and humid. Bowlers would seek to bowl fast, but with as short a run-up as possible. Batsmen were keen to hit boundaries, so as to minimise the need to run. In that sense, they brought a little of the feel of Twenty20, long before its time. A really good six would occasionally go right over the church roof and land in the vicarage garden. We had a good garden – watered by treated effluent, brought round each week in a tanker."

Away from the game and the necessity of avoiding being brained by cricket balls while tending to their rosebushes, Nicholas and his wife Ann were kept very busy during their time on Ascension. It's clear that even nearly two decades on he still looks back on his time there fondly.

"There was such a range of work. I was also the lay advocate defending all those who came to court; Ann did much of her pastoral work as manager of the video and sports shop and so on. But one cannot be giving out spiritually and pastorally for too long without renewing contact with the rest of the Church. It would have been indulgent to have stayed longer, but it was a great experience while it lasted. We miss Ascension hugely."

The current state of Ascension cricket is hard to discern. Canon Turner told me that the website of the island newspaper *The Islander*, which he used to edit, has no mention of cricket in its archives after the year 2000. Perhaps the clerical begonias are now safe from being peppered by an artillery of little red missiles, but if that's the case it would be a terrible shame. There's something strangely comforting about the thought of cricket being played all the way out there on a big lump of volcanic rock hundreds of miles from anywhere in the choppy waters of the south Atlantic, and one hopes that the game continues and flourishes.

For one thing, on the eastern side of the island, the opposite side to the capital Georgetown, there is a Cricket Valley. For another, the island has a first-class cricket legacy to perpetuate: William Delacombe is the only Ascension-born cricketer ever to feature in the first-class game. His father, Captain William Addis Delacombe of the Royal Marines, had been posted to Georgetown and was there when young William arrived in 1860. His stay on the island was brief: the family returned to England soon afterwards when William senior was appointed Chief Constable of Derby. William junior would grow to a strapping 6ft 5ins, become a keen cricketer and turn out on ten occasions for Derbyshire, where he also held the post of club secretary until 1908. His greatest cricket moment, however, came not for Derbyshire but at Dunstable in 1897 when, while playing for the Incogniti against L. C. R. Thring's XI, he took all ten wickets, including a hat-trick.

The 1912 *Wisden* obituary of William Delacombe noted that "although he was not a great cricketer, he was certainly a useful one".

AZERBAIJAN

In April 1995 a small but determined band established the Baku Cricket Club, the first in the Caucasus. Five years on, a multi-ethnic collection of 25–30 cricketers play every Sunday from May to October on a football pitch. The first one used was far from ideal: covered with rubber matting taken from a running track, it had short boundaries and a rough outfield littered with dog dirt. Two years ago, however, the club got the opportunity to play on a surface more conducive to cricket; it was still used for football but with bigger boundaries and better grass (though inclined to be over-watered by the zealous groundsman). And the players have a proper mat. That the BCC is playing at all owes much to its hard-working first honorary secretary Caroline Adams, who was a regular spectator along with her cairn terriers Benji and Susie. Initially almost all the players came from the Indian subcontinent. The first Azerbaijani player was a 13-year-old called Emin. He was a natural batsman, rarely playing a cross-batted shot, and was being coached by the Pakistani chargé d'affaires Raja Masood, and Lutful Kabir, then head of the Azerbaijani branch of the charity Save the Children. Emin enjoyed playing, but, after six weeks or so he was set upon by a group of youths. He came to training only once after that, by which time he had been transformed from a slim, unimposing figure into a broad-shouldered, tall young man. When asked where he had been during the previous two months, he replied, "I've been learning karate." *Alum Bati*, **Wisden 2000**

When Azerbaijan earned its independence in 1991 it wasn't long before western nations were casting lecherous leers – expertly disguised behind coquettish glances – at the fledgling nation's oil reserves. In 1994 a contract was signed allowing a number of oil companies access to the black gold beneath Azeri territory, most of them British. With so many Brits arriving on the shores of the Caspian

Sea it wasn't long before themed shops and pubs – with names like Chaplin's and Shakespeare's – began appearing all over Baku (one Azeri publication sought to introduce the concept of the English pub to locals, pointing out that "it is not obligatory to drink beer, but pub landlords say that beer is the cornerstone of the business. Beer is an ideal drink in pubs since it is served in large glasses and people can talk while they are drinking."). Inevitably, cricket was not far behind. The driving force behind the game's inception was Alum Bati, a London-born lawyer who was, among other things, a legal adviser to the British Ambassador to Azerbaijan. Bati helped to organise Azerbaijan's first international match, against a Rest of the World XI captained by the British ambassador Andrew Tucker in 2002, but in that year's *Wisden* he was lamenting the "miserable turnout" of players for matches. A year later there were "encouraging numbers of Azeri cricketers", but hints of financial problems suggested dark clouds forming over cricket in Baku. Indeed, by 2011 it appeared the Baku club was defunct and, while ad hoc games of cricket are still played, the future of Azeri cricket looks uncertain.

AUSTRIA

There was drama in the final of the Austrian Open League in September, Lord's CC triumphed over Pakistan CC thanks to A. Ajay, who took the first recorded hat-trick in Austrian championship cricket. An English touring team visited Vienna in May, and formally opened Austria's first full-sized ground at nearby Seebarn. France then arrived to play the first two internationals there, but Austria won both matches – the first by just two runs after setting a target of 301. Another new cricket ground was inaugurated at Velden in September, becoming the third purpose-built venue in the country. Two of them are surrounded by breathtaking Alpine mountains, and the last, Seebarn, is in the centre of one of Austria's wine regions. *Andrew Simpson-Parker,* **Wisden 1997**

BAHRAIN

Cricket thrives in Bahrain. The island state has a population of 500,000 and boasts about 50 teams, playing most Fridays in temperatures that can approach 50°C. The vast majority of the players are usually from the Indian subcontinent, and those Bahrainis that take part are usually either naturalised immigrants or have been educated abroad. The game came to Bahrain with expatriate oil-workers in the 1930s when the first wells were spudded in. The oldest club is in the oil village of Awali, and it is an oasis of cricketing comfort, complete with cucumber sandwiches. This is the exception, however, as the facilities at the other grounds vary from the rudimentary to the non-existent. The outfields are desert; sometimes rolled, sometimes not; sometimes sandy, sometimes concrete-hard; but always unpredictable. The best wickets are concrete strips covered with coir; Awali use a green composite mat designed for use as a swimming-pool surround. There is not a blade of grass to be seen anywhere. Nevertheless, the best four or five teams among the 16 that make up the Bahrain Cricket Association include some very strong players, mostly from Pakistan. In recent years the BCA Select XI has beaten a touring Pakistan International Airlines XI containing eight current or recent Pakistani Test players, and narrowly lost to a strong MCC side out to celebrate Awali CC's 60th season. Desert cricket is an unforgettable experience – and camels really do sometimes wander across the pitch. *Guy Parker,* **Wisden 1997**

BERMUDA

The euphoria surrounding Bermuda's qualification for the 2007 World Cup dissipated when the annual Cup Match, described by the *Royal Gazette* as "the island's most cherished sporting institution", was disfigured by a punch-up. Cup Match, a two-day game between Bermuda's biggest clubs, Somerset and St George, was being staged for the 102nd time in July 2005 when St George's fast bowler, George O'Brien, allegedly punched Somerset batsman Stephen Outerbridge on the jaw, after Outerbridge had apparently spat at him. O'Brien took 11 wickets in his team's first Cup win since 2000, watched each day by 7,000, more than a tenth of Bermuda's population. Both men were forced to issue public apologies, and St George's skipper, Herbie Bascome, was sacked as the national Under-19 coach. The Bermuda Cricket Board did, however, send O'Brien for winter training in Brisbane (as well as an anger-management course) and named both men in their provisional World Cup squad, along with David Hemp, the Bermuda-born Glamorgan batsman. **Wisden 2006**

BHUTAN

For centuries, none but the most intrepid made it through the steep mountain passes to reach proudly independent Bhutan in the heart of the Himalayas. The national sport of archery protected the country against invaders, but the Bhutanese were helpless before the onslaught of television. Starting in 2001, Indian TV started threading its way through the highlands and with it came an appreciation of movies, soap operas – and cricket. "Cricket caught on just because of Star TV and Doordarshan," says the former Indian all-rounder Roger Binny, who now coaches in Bhutan. Out of a population of 2.2 million only 200 or so are active cricketers. The ground in the capital of Thimphu (2,300m, or 7,500ft, above sea level) is small. And the season is short: it is a cold and windy place. But the children from privileged families are sent to study in India. There they learn the fame and bring it home, where cricket acquires a uniquely Bhutanese flavour. Players bow their heads in supplication to the cricketing gods before taking the field. "We do not pray for victory," says national team captain Dhamber Singh Gurung. "We pray for each other to give our best and to emerge complete from the competition." The Dechephu Lhakhang temple in Thimphu is the spiritual home of Bhutan cricket, and cricketers visit before every tournament to invoke the protecting deities. The team has had some success, beating Myanmar in the 2006 ACC Trophy. But Bhutan is no place for bowlers; at that altitude, the ball simply flies off the bat. One bowler, Phuntso Wangchuk, exasperated by being hammered, has resorted to storing his cricket balls in his father's humidor in order to make them "heavier". However, he may yet have to give up bowling for cheroot-smoking. *Shahriar Khan*, **Wisden 2007**

With its national aim of finding a balance between increasing modernisation and spiritual well-being, Bhutan is almost a metaphor for modern cricket in sovereign state form. While cricket is engaged in a battle for its soul in the face of rampant commercialism and relentless moneymaking, so Bhutan tries to balance a need to keep up with global developments without succumbing to the raging consumerism that its location ensured was kept at bay until recently.

The remote Himalayan nation has since 1971 measured its economic success not solely via figures on a balance sheet but on a scale of Gross National Happiness. In the light of this it's a wonder that cricket has only developed in recent years.

"When people overwork and go into debt to buy ever more goods and pay the bills, they get more stressed," the Bhutanese prime minister Jigme Thinley told the United Nations in 2012. "Working, producing and consuming less is not only good for nature but gives us more time to enjoy each other." No wonder, then, that cricket is consistently increasing in popularity despite Bhutan being one of the poorest nations in the world and the lack of even a full-sized cricket ground in the country.

Fitting though Bhutanese principles are for the propagation of the game, it's only very recently that cricket has gained any kind of foothold. The main reason for that is that television didn't arrive in Bhutan until 1999. Even then, unless you were fortunate enough to have a satellite dish – an expensive accessory in such a poor country – for two years anyone switching on their television would generally find little else but endless re-runs of Bhutanese royal occasions. Then, in 2001, Indian channels were made widely available, meaning Bollywood films, Indian soap operas – and cricket.

From that standing start, in little over a decade cricket has made incredible progress: in its first major tournament, the 2004 ACC Trophy in Malaysia, a victory over Iran helped Bhutan reach the quarter-finals where, although they were hammered by Oman, who reached their target of 71 in less than five overs, Bhutan gave a decent account of themselves despite their chronic inexperience.

Roger Binny, a veteran of India's World Cup win in 1983, became the Asian Cricket Council's development officer for the region later that year, and made such an impression in Bhutan that he appeared on a postage stamp in 2007.

"The thing I liked there was the enthusiasm," said Binny recently. "Bhutan's women's team in particular was pretty decent. We generally worked with schoolchildren and age-group teams and they had shown a lot of improvement."

His successor, the former Sri Lankan pace bowler Rumesh Ratnayake, concurred. "These cricketers embody the true amateur spirit, they play at quite some cost to themselves for the pure love of the game," he said. "Some sponsors are coming in but the amounts of money are so small that a club would be hard-pressed to make the money stretch to a cricket bat. And yet when they win a domestic tournament it's like the biggest thing in their lives."

One of the main reasons for the growth of cricket in Bhutan is the limitless enthusiasm of Damber Singh Gurung. He grew up in a remote part of the country but had made the seven-hour journey to Thimphu in his late teens in 1999, and while there managed to see one of these new-fangled televisions everyone had been talking about. Fortunately for Bhutanese cricket, the set Gurung happened to park in front of was showing a match from the 1999 World Cup. Gurung was hooked instantly, he began playing, organised Bhutan's first cricket tournament the following year, played for and captained the national side, and is now the fresh, passionate face of the Bhutan Cricket Council.

In some ways his job – officially titled Coaching Co-ordinator – is a straightforward one as the Bhutanese mindset and the game of cricket seem well-suited. The introspection and spiritual depth of Buddhism, the Bhutanese national religion, makes cricket seem a perfect fit. Also, while archery is by far the most popular sport – every village in the country has an archery field – most traditional pastimes in Bhutan involve throwing things, from darts to large stones. However, there are problems too. Television has also brought football, which competes for the attention of Bhutanese youth, while the monsoon season means that there are only three months each year when cricket can be played. In such a mountainous country, even finding places large enough to play on is a serious issue.

"They're either too small or they do not exist," Gurung said of Bhutanese cricket grounds in 2011. "In the south of Bhutan there are a few grounds, but in the north and the capital Thimphu there aren't very many. Thimphu is already very crowded. There are a lot of people who want to play cricket but don't have anywhere to play the game."

Gurung estimates that there are some 5,000 cricketers in Bhutan (*Wisden* overestimated the total population somewhat: it's certainly nearer 750,000 than 2.2 million) and remains determined to grow that number. In 2013 he implemented a new development plan designed to get more experienced coaches helping the national sides at all levels and training coaches to go out into the countryside and give youngsters a decent grounding in the game. (Bhutan is overwhelmingly rural: the capital Thimphu is roughly the size of Redditch, while most of the population of this agricultural nation live in remote villages surrounded by farmland.)

It's not all sweetness and light in Bhutan, however. In the early 1990s some 100,000 ethnic Nepalis fled the country after a 1988 census labelled them illegal immigrants, sparking a wave of violence. There were even bombings as recently as the government elections of 2008. The status of the Nepalese refugees remains unclear, meaning relations between Bhutan and Nepal can be tricky. Damber Singh Gurung himself played in the first encounter between the two national sides in 2003, but would probably rather forget it. Although he took the first three wickets to fall, the Nepalese racked up a whopping 397 for eight from their 50 overs, and in reply the overwhelmed Bhutanese were bowled out for 44. To date Bhutan have never beaten Nepal at any level in men's or women's cricket. The Bhutanese take it on the chin though as they are, of course, a very spiritual side.

BOTSWANA

Cricket has struggled to gain a foothold in Botswana ever since the construction of the Bulawayo–Mafeking railway line brought it here in the 19th century, but things are looking up. Although the game had occasionally survived in private primary schools, generations were lost to softball and football. Now though, thanks to frequent broadcasting of South Africa's matches and significant development work, there are around 30 primary and secondary schools regularly playing in an informal league. The national team, including four native Botswanans, surprised both Kenyan and Namibian development sides before losing the final of the Africa Cup to South Africa in Zambia. And the Under-15s, similarly made up of nationals and expatriates, were competitive against Namibia, Zambia, Malawi and Lesotho. Courses sponsored by the ICC have produced nearly 80 Level-1 qualified coaches. We are also proud that the capital, Gaborone, has one of the continent's few floodlit cricket grounds outside South Africa, even if stray cattle and the odd donkey need to be shooed off before play. More needs to be done: Botswana has fewer than 400 players using just 30 pitches.

Jack Sands, **Wisden 2003**

For a country the size of France nestled between cricket nations like South Africa, Zimbabwe and Namibia, not to mention its history as a British protectorate between 1885 and 1966, Botswana's cricket heritage is surprisingly flimsy. The first mention of the game dates back to 1879, possibly with the arrival of European gold prospectors, but it's only in recent years that cricket has really started to take hold. Promising showings at international level earned Botswana an upgrade to ICC Associate Member status in 2005 just four years after becoming an Affiliate, but the nation's cricket resources have more recently been directed towards developing the game in schools. The 7,000 children receiving coaching in schools across the country, even in the parched north of the Kalahari Desert, is quite a leap in a decade from the hardy bunch of 400 Botswanan cricketers of 2003. Women's cricket is proving particularly popular: in 2011

Botswana finished second in the African Cricket Association's Under-19 tournament despite the team having an average age of just 14.

BRUNEI DARUSSALAM

Alas, a large window broken by a well-struck straight six resulted in cricket being banned from the Shell Recreation Ground. Two years earlier the siting of soccer goals 15 yards from the bat at short midwicket had added an interesting dimension to the game. Although not proving as inconvenient as one might imagine, it was a sign of things to come. Cricket in Brunei is now restricted to the Panaga ground, and is down to five teams including the now-homeless Shell Recreation Club. An early-season match between Panaga and Manggis provided an astonishing result. Manggis won the toss and elected to bat, as their Pakistani players had been attending a function in honour of a visiting government minister and were due to arrive a little late. Unfortunately, they lost seven wickets for seven and were thus all out before the missing players could arrive. Panaga won by eight wickets, and went on to win the league. Royal Brunei Yacht Club, as usual, won the Galfar Knockout Cup. Towards the end of the season, Brunei defeated Sabah and Sarawak to win the Borneo Cup, which Sabah had held for the previous two years. *Derek Thursby*, **Wisden 2001**

BULGARIA

Saif Rehman is the pioneering force of Bulgarian cricket, a soap star, semi-finalist in *Bulgaria's Got Talent* – and now symbol of egalitarianism in his adopted country. During the Communist era, Bulgarian disabled children were often hidden from view by their families, or abandoned in state institutions. While there has been undoubted progress, some attitudes have proved hard to shake. A 2008 investigation by Europe's highest social-rights body criticised the Bulgarian government for failing to provide disabled children with an education. Two years later, it was reported that 166 had died from neglect in care homes over the previous decade. Rehman, 39, originally from Pakistan, was deeply upset at what he saw, and vowed to bring cricket to the less fortunate. In January 2012, he introduced a group of children from Sofia to table cricket, a miniature table-top version of the game for six players. By November, around 100 Bulgarians aged six to 17 with cerebral palsy, Down's Syndrome or other disabilities were playing table cricket, and a national championship was held. "We've had great results," said Rehman. "Doctors have told me that a 16-year-old opened his hand for the first time after he started playing, because he was getting movement in it and was so determined to play." The widespread praise for the initiative inside Bulgaria persuaded Rehman to begin coaching a national squad of blind cricketers, whom he hopes to take on a tour to England in 2013. Germany and Spain are the only other countries in continental Europe to play any official disability cricket. "My ambition is to form a disability cricket league and encourage it in nearby countries," Rehman declared. "This is my duty." *Tristan Lavalette*, **Wisden 2013**

CAMBODIA

The Phnom Penh Cricket Club was formed in early 1999 and a small group of Indians are reported to be playing regularly on the beautiful playground at the North Bridge International School. Initially a tennis ball was used because of fears of having to use the poor Cambodian medical facilities, but the members have now become bold enough to play with a proper ball. **Wisden 2000**

CANADA

British explorers Matt Coates and Matthew Hancock were forced to give up their attempt to walk to the Magnetic North Pole in March 2005 after Hancock suffered frostbite. However, just before being rescued, they did succeed in playing what is claimed to be the most northerly cricket ever, on the Arctic ice close to the Reindeer Peninsula (78° 45′ N, 104° 03′ W). "We managed to get an inflatable bat and stumps," Coates said. "Unfortunately, it was minus 45°C at the time, and they broke into a thousand pieces. So we turned the ski poles into stumps and used a ski as a bat. We did have a real cricket ball and a snowman for a fielder. Matt Hancock played one really beautiful sweep shot, even with his frostbite." **Wisden 2006**

An achievement though it unquestionably was to have a game of cricket way up at high latitude on the northern tip of the Svalbard archipelago, not least with frostbite and using a ski as a bat, alas for Matt Coates and Matthew Hancock they were still a good way short of playing the most northerly cricket in the world. Around 600 miles short, in fact. Indeed, there are at least three recorded instances of cricket being played at the North Pole itself.

Hancock is now the MP for West Suffolk where, on his website, he still claims to have played the "most northerly recorded game of cricket". As someone who can't play a sweep shot under any circumstances, let alone with frostbitten fingers and using a ski for a bat, I'm not about to belittle his achievement on that 2005 expedition, but – frostbite or not – until you've played your trademark sweep shot at the very top of the world itself then your northerly cricket claims are always going to ring a little hollow.

The first game of north-polar cricket took place in 1976 when the British nuclear submarine HMS *Sovereign* broke through the ice, a hatch opened, members of the crew emerged blinking carrying bat, stumps and ball, and a makeshift game of cricket took place. There is photographic evidence too: unable to drive the stumps into the ice the sailors had piled snow around them instead, and it seems a real wooden bat was used. For all that, and for all the smiles of those involved however, it looked a dark, cold and pretty miserable affair. Still, if I'd been cooped up for weeks in a massive tin can under the sea, a game of cricket in the dark in temperatures so far below freezing they'd need some kind of diagram to guide them back up again would doubtless seem like the last word in hedonism by comparison.

It would be 15 years until the North Pole saw cricket again, and this time the top of the world would see its first international encounter. In 1991 the British submarine HMS *Tireless* and her American counterpart the USS *Prago* both surfaced at the Pole and contested a cricket match on a matting wicket brought along especially for the occasion. A crowd of around 100 fellow servicemen watched as the British won the game, largely due to the fact that the American team didn't really have much of an idea of what cricket actually involved.

Most recently, in April 2008, the Indian navy produced arguably the most impressive piece of North Pole cricket to date. Rather than turning up all cosy and warm in a big namby-pamby submarine, ten members of the Indian navy skied there, and in doing so completed their impressive hat-trick of skiing both poles and climbing Mount Everest. While there they encountered a party of British explorers led by David Hempleman-Adams and, as is customary when two disparate groups of people meet in the middle of nowhere at the top of the world, a cricket match was hastily arranged.

The quality on show was not bad either, considering they were using a plastic spade for a bat, ski poles for stumps and a pair of old woollen socks rolled up and swathed with tape as a ball, not to mention the trifling matter of it being 40 degrees below zero. A thrilling five-overs-a-side encounter followed, from which the Indians emerged victorious by just one run. When you've skied to both poles and climbed the world's highest mountain, it's probably no surprise that you have the steely determination to close out the tightest of finishes and make sure it goes in your favour.

Hancock and Coates may not quite have matched these achievements, but they did manage to outdo the northerliness of the only other notable cricket occasions to take place on the Svalbard Archipelago, including a remarkable achievement by one of the greatest players in the game's history. The first occasion was in 1885 when four British ships were moored in Recherche Bay, the *Active*, the *Calypso*, the *Volage* and the *Ruby*. Two teams were selected and a game arranged in which the combined ranks of the *Active* and the *Calypso* triumphed. An old mining settlement on the southern headland of the bay is called Calypsobyen to this day. If the outcome of a cricket match results in the location being named in honour of the winners it puts shoving a few cinders into an old urn into perspective, if you ask me.

The best story of cricket on Svalbard, however, involves one of the greatest cricketers who ever lived, Alfred Shaw. In 1894 he was in Svalbard – or Spitsbergen as it was known then – cruising on board the yacht of his friend Lord Sheffield. Shaw is quoted in his memoirs *Alfred Shaw, Cricketer: His Career and Reminiscences* as recalling: "We were nestling in the bosom of a peaceful ice fjord at midnight, with the Arctic sun at its lowest point lighting up the snow-clad mountains and the magnificent glaciers around us. It was Lord Sheffield who at this weird hour and in these eerie surroundings suggested a cricket match. The idea was promptly taken up by all on board. Wickets were pitched, a ball improvised and at about a quarter to twelve on the night of August 12, 1894, this strange game commenced. Of course, I had to bowl and Lord Sheffield opened the batting. Between a quarter to twelve and half past twelve I had bowled out practically all the gentlemen passengers and officers, certainly 40 persons all told. It will be seen that it was pretty quick work from the bowler's point of view."

Shaw was two weeks shy of his 52nd birthday. He'd play another three seasons of first-class cricket.

There should be a special mention here also for the earliest recorded game to take place above the Arctic Circle. In 1823 Captain William Parry was sitting out the winter waiting for the ice that had encased his two ships HMS *Hecla* and HMS *Fury* since the previous autumn to break up in order to continue his quest to find the North-West Passage. They were wintering three degrees above the Arctic Circle near Igoolik in what's now the Canadian province of Nunavut, and by March the endless winter darkness was at last being conquered by the returning sun, and a distinct glow was seeping over the horizon. The exploration party was in understandably good spirits and reacted accordingly.

Parry wrote in his journal on March 8, 1823, of how "the weather was now so pleasant, and the temperature in the sun so comfortable to the feelings when a shelter could be found from the wind, that we set up various games for the people, such as cricket, foot-ball, and quoits, which some of them played for many hours during the day."

CAYMAN ISLANDS

The 1995 season was dominated by Wesley Gidson, captain of the Cayman Brac Second Division team, who scored 652 in six innings, averaging 217.33 with a top score of 237 not out – and took 21 wickets at seven each. Cayman Brac is the second-largest of the Cayman Islands, and competition with the main island, Grand Cayman, only started in 1994. The highlight of the year was a festival involving several West Indian Test players who played a match with 27 sixes, watched by 2,000 spectators. Cricket began here in the 1960s; the pitch is a rubber mat laid on asphalt. *Jimmy Powell,* **Wisden 1996**

CHILE

In the last two years cricket in Chile has undergone a revival. In 1999 it was reintroduced in several schools, with 50 or so boys and girls now enjoying the game. Though Chilean cricket has dwindled since its heyday in the 1920s, the game has been kept alive and is now thriving, thanks to the generosity of the Prince of Wales Country Club, which offers its splendid ground at the foot of the Andes to cricketers every summer. This offer is currently being taken up by some 50 enthusiasts, mainly British expats with a smattering of other cricketing nationalities, a few Chileans, plus the odd US baseball player. The club schedules about 20 games per season, mostly intra-club matches, with occasional visits from UK and Australian teams and a very welcome annual visit from the Argentine Cricket Association. Whenever the Antarctic survey ship HMS *Endurance* docks in Valparaiso a game is arranged, thus taking us back to 1829 and the very origins of cricket in Chile – when teams from two Royal Navy ships met. Recent visitors include Rosslyn Cricket Club, Old Merchant Taylors', the Old Bedfordians, Stowe School and a Stockbrokers' XI. Until the Stockbrokers came, only the occasional Australian had been seen fielding with a glass (or more likely a bottle) of beer in his hand. However, some of the Stockbrokers astounded their opponents by going out to field with a gin and tonic in each hand. MCC are sending a team in 2001; they are not expected to match this. *Anthony Adams*, **Wisden 2001**

This was Chile's second appearance in Cricket Round the World, and its tone is markedly different to the faintly Eeyorish 1996 entry that lamented how there was only one cricket club in Chile, barely 30 players and that the only visitors of note had been Bath Schools. A year after this 2001 entry, however, *Wisden* reported the formation of the Chilean Cricket Association, that the MCC had visited as part of a tour of South America, that Santiago boasted four teams, and that plans were afoot to revive cricket in Valparaiso, where the game in Chile was born. Affiliate Membership of the ICC followed a year later.

Details of the 1829 match between two Royal Navy ships at Valparaiso are hard to verify. Now a thriving city of more than a quarter of a million people, in 1829 Valparaiso was a small port town and the base for the new Chilean navy. An 1830 drawing of the town reveals a few buildings scattered over some steep-looking hills – any prospective cricketers might have had a job finding a piece of ground flat enough to accommodate a half-decent game. It's possible that one of the Royal Navy vessels was the frigate HMS *Seringatapam* under the command of William Waldegrave, which was certainly in the area at the time, but otherwise the vessels – and hence the names of the teams – remain a mystery.

However, it seems that the 1829 match wasn't the first recorded cricket match in Chile after all. In fact it wasn't even the first cricket match in Valparaiso. According to Volume 28 of Josiah Conder's whopping 30-book series *The Modern Traveller: A Popular Description, Geographical, Historical and Topographical, Of The Various Countries Of The Globe*, published in 1829, cricket was being played 11 years before that. In 1818 Lord Thomas Cochrane, a famous naval captain from the Napoleonic Wars (and quite a character: both Horatio Hornblower and Jack Aubrey were based at least in part on Cochrane), arrived in Valparaiso to take charge of the Chilean Navy in their war of independence with Spain, having been forced out of Britain following his conviction for involvement in a stock-exchange fraud. He arrived in November 1818, was immediately granted Chilean citizenship and appointed the nation's first vice-admiral. His arrival was marked with "grand dinners, cricket-matches, races and picnic parties" that apparently "rendered Valparaiso unusually gay".

Still, whether the first match was played in 1829 or 1818 or even earlier, Chilean cricket is now in the twilight of its second century even if it took until 1860 for the first official club to be formed, fittingly in Valparaiso.

By the 1920s Chilean cricket was thriving mainly thanks to British expats involved in the nitrates industry. Clubs sprang up in the capital Santiago, including one at the Prince of Wales Country Club in 1925, taking its name from the future Edward VIII, who had officially opened the ground. The Prince of Wales complex would become effectively the home of Chilean cricket (the 1996 *Wisden* reported that membership at that time cost $500,000 – fortunately the cricketers were given use of the facilities without having to take out membership). Pelham Warner led a touring side to Chile in the 1920s, and the nation's cricket pedigree was boosted when Freddie

Brown, who was born in Peru and went to St Peter's School in Santiago, captained both Northamptonshire and England in the 1950s.

After the Second World War British expats began to leave and the game dwindled steadily throughout the 1950s. There were still pockets of enthusiasm and activity in the country and Argentina continued to be regular tourists. In March 1954 the Argentineans lost a thrilling game by four runs, a match arguably more notable for being the only recorded game played by the distinguished English historian Eric Hobsbawm. He had relatives in Chile, and it was presumably while visiting them that he was invited to turn out for the Prince of Wales Country Club. A member of the Communist Party of Great Britain at the time, Hobsbawm made an incongruous recruit to what was clearly a pretty lah-di-dah cricketing set-up. Batting at No. 10 he made one in the first innings and what turned out to be a crucial 15 in the second. He took one catch.

It was the first Argentinean tour of Chile in 1893 that is most worthy of note here, though. For a start, the Argentina team had to cross the Andes by mule, a journey of three and a half days.

"It is quite possible that in the future the lasting reconciliation between Argentina and Chile will be attributed to a few cricketers, accompanied in this endeavour by beautiful ladies, who departed from Buenos Aires on Monday, November 13, 1893," hyped the Argentinean newspaper *La Nacion,* breathlessly. The paper goes on to list the names of the pride of Argentine cricket, all of which are distinctly English, right down to the *Times of Argentina* correspondent travelling with them, Mr R. H. Morgan.

"The party's attire and travelling implements were the subject of much hilarity and jokes," continued *La Nacion.* "The extravagant headgear, the goggles to protect the eyes from dust, the baggage, truly Noah's Arks in which toothbrushes were dancing among flannel trousers, books and cigarettes, the entire proverbial luggage of English travellers."

They took the train as far as Mendoza at the foot of the Andes before transferring to mules and crossing the mountains into Chile. The hardship and ridicule seemed to be worth it, though – not only did the Argentina team win all three games against Chile, they also managed to win a football match, a tennis match and a billiards contest too. The three-day yomp back across the mountains would have been a distinctly happy one.

CHRISTMAS ISLAND

A crowd of about 200 looks on as an Afghan bowler sends down a delivery on the rolled dirt wicket to a Sri Lankan batsman, while the fielders – both Afghans and Sri Lankans – are ready to pounce. The scores are recorded studiously, for errors cannot be afforded in this vigorously contested limited-overs game. Behind the razor wire of the Christmas Island Detention Centre in the Indian Ocean, cricket provides a vital degree of normality for the lives of the detainees, who stay for around three months on this Australian territory while visa applications are processed. This game is not an isolated event: there are organised competitions contested by up to ten teams, usually of mixed nationalities. Neither is the sport confined to the detention centre. The staff take part in the occasional match against the Christmas Island Cricket and Sporting Club, whose eclectic civilian membership play up to six games a year. The club organises most of the sporting activity on this island of nearly 1,500 people, including Australian Rules, touch football, soccer and softball. But cricket remains the primary sport, and the Department of Immigration and SERCO (the security operators) work with the cricket club to ensure there are enough opportunities to play for those in detention. The multicultural nature of the population is reflected in the club's membership: Australian, English, Malay, Chinese – and even an Inuit. The Sri Lankans, meanwhile, bring

flair. One has an action like the country's slingy Test bowler Lasith Malinga; another kisses the ball before each delivery. Last year the club, which recently celebrated its 50th anniversary, included matches against the staff of the detention centre, visiting Royal Australian Navy ships and teams from Cocos Island, 900km to the south-west. It also holds the Coconut Ashes, an annual clash between "chalkies" (teachers) and the locals. The community oval has its own peculiar features: it is mostly surrounded by jungle, which makes losing balls something of a hazard, while fog and low cloud can get in the way too, as games take place on top of "The Rock", as the island is referred to, a full 300m above sea level.
Tony Munro and Rhett Bowden, **Wisden 2010**

COLOMBIA

Cricket is not endemic in the High Andes. Indeed, it is so alien to local culture that Colombian customs reputedly impounded a priceless shipment of bats and balls from Venezuela some years ago as "dangerous, possibly subversive material". Bogota is a challenge for the bowler. At 8,300ft above sea level, anyone trying to bowl medium-fast soon runs out of puff, and the ball will not swing much in the thin dry air. A spinner gets a little more help from our new Astroturf than from the old matting we had until 1994, and the batsman does not have an easy time. The field is kikuyu grass: the ball will not skim the surface, and must be hit dangerously high to reach the boundary. Cricket's popularity in Colombia has ebbed and flowed depending on the numbers of expatriates. It was first regularly played by Shell employees in the mid-1950s. Since then English schoolmasters, Scottish accountants and Pakistani bankers have come and gone, and now oil – this time BP – provides most of the players. However, it is difficult to get teams together more than once or twice a month. We would very much welcome any touring side with the ambition to do something different. *Anthony Letts*, **Wisden 1997**

DEMOCRATIC REPUBLIC OF CONGO

Goma Stadium in the eastern Congo (formerly Zaire) is not the most obvious setting for a one-day international, however unofficial. In March 2004 it was the venue for a match between India and Pakistan, as intensely contested as if it were in Karachi or Kolkata. The players were members of the 12,000-strong peacekeeping mission, which is trying to end the long war in Congo. The outfield was black, due to lava from the eruption of Mount Nyriangongo in 2002. The boundary markers were old gun-boxes covered in gleaming white. The umpire's job was less to worry about the lbw law (which was interpreted liberally) than to stop UN soldiers from non-cricketing countries walking behind the arm, or even on the wicket. In the words of one Swedish soldier: "The UN warned me about gorillas attacking us, but not cricket balls!" The match was a 20-over slog so that the soldiers could return to barracks in time to start the night patrols: genuine nightwatchmen. India won, having avoided any attacks by gorillas. A Pakistani outfielder, however, had to make a run for it as a herd of goats from the prison farm dashed across the outfield, followed by the prisoners and their guards. *David Turner*, **Wisden 2005**

COOK ISLANDS

Over the past three years I have had the pleasure of assisting with cricket development in the Cook Islands, and I now coach the national team, which is a magical experience: the players possess what you might call raw potential, but in terms of entertainment they are definitely first-class. A musical bunch, their powerful rendition of the national anthem can be quite moving. For a small nation with only 11,000 potential players the Cook Islands have performed remarkably well in recent times, climbing to No. 3 in the ICC's East Asia Pacific rankings. The annual trials between the two main cricket islands of Rarotonga and Aitutaki form an important part of that development, by giving hopefuls the chance to stake their claim for national selection. Our most recent trials were held in Tautu on Aitutaki. The pitch there is one of seven concrete pits on the island which are sunk below the surface and covered with sand during the winter to allow rugby and soccer to be played over the top. In the summer the sand is cleared away to reveal a reasonable playing surface, although most of these pits have been down for 70 years. And so, with the Tautu strip showing its age, some overnight repairs were required. The locals got to work and placed cement in the various cracks, but their decision to use a flip-flop to screed the concrete rather than a trowel meant conditions looked like being a challenge for the batsmen. However, once the pitch was covered with a carpet that had previously rested in the aisle of the local church, the surface played well. During my last visit I played in a club game in Aitutaki, which – with eight club sides, many of them containing two men's teams as well as women and junior XIs – is the local cricket stronghold. A lagoon, around 30m away, forms the boundary on one side, while the island's main road runs within the other. I managed to take a couple of catches, one of them as I sprinted down the middle of the road while trying to keep one eye on the ball and the other on traffic. The local batsmen treated my off-spin with respect for a while, before despatching me into the lagoon. Fortunately a plastic-coated ball is used, so a short swim is normally enough for play to resume. An early leg-before decision ended my stay with the bat. Let's just say that umpiring will be on the agenda for my next visit. *Grant Bradburn*, **Wisden 2008**

Running a cricket club can be a nightmare sometimes. Players crying off at the last minute after going down with a sudden and severe case of cock-and-bull story, sorting out match fees, organising lifts; it's a pretty time-consuming business. Imagine how those problems multiply when you're running a league, then a cricket association, then a national governing body. Then imagine doing that in the Cook Islands.

There's less than 100 square miles of territory in the Cook Islands, situated in the southern Pacific Ocean north-east of New Zealand. One hundred square miles doesn't sound much, but that's divided among 15 islands. And those 15 islands are spread across 690,000 square miles of the Pacific Ocean. There are fewer than 20,000 people living on the Cook Islands – nearly three-quarters of them on Rarotonga. Yet, despite the sheer geography of the place, cricket is thriving. Indeed, according to the Cook Islands Cricket Association, a quarter of the whole population plays some kind of cricket.

The game arrived on the islands at the turn of the 20th century when missionaries arrived bearing bats as well as bibles. Rarotonga Cricket Club was founded in 1910, and the game was popular with expats, but went into a gradual decline from the 1950s until there were only around half a dozen clubs left.

The new millennium brought new hope, however. ICC affiliation was achieved in 2000, and progress was speeded up by the appointment of a full-time administrator in 2009. As a result cricket is thriving again. The national team is making steady progress – especially in the Twenty20 format, for which the islanders seem to have a big-hitting aptitude – and participation reaches levels that belie the far-flung nature of the islands and put to shame nations whose infrastructure is far more geared to the game.

One of the furthest flung of all the islands is the coral atoll Pukapuka, more than 700 miles from Rarotonga. There are barely 500 people living on three islets that huddle around a lagoon; barely a square mile of territory, yet Pukapuka is the most cricket-mad part of the Cooks. The game as we know it has only been introduced in the last decade: what the Pukapukans play, indeed, what they refer to as their national sport, is a version of cricket that reflects how the atoll is closer in location, spirit and culture to Samoa than Rarotonga.

The game is called *kirikiti*. It looks a great deal like cricket, but this game has a distinctly Pacific flavour. There are batsmen, there are bowlers, there are fielders. There are even wicketkeepers: one at each end. The stumps are chest-high and the bats have more in common with Samoan war clubs than lovingly crafted willow wands. The *kirikiti* bat is a metre or more long, and three-sided. It's made from the wood of the kapok tree, and players develop a close relationship with it: most are painted in patterns of bright colour. The ball is made from hardened rubber, and the idea is for the batsman to hit it as far as he can. There is no limit to the amount of players on each side, nor is there any kind of restriction on age or gender: many games are effectively village against village – the whole village, man, woman and child. In the past, games have been known to go on for days, and there is a definite festival feel to the occasion: one local rule has it that if the home side fails to prepare enough food they immediately forfeit the match.

It's a curious game, and it's played in a curious place. Pukapuka was named the Dangerous Islands by a British naval captain who found his ship unable to land in the mid-18th century thanks to the reefs that surround the atoll. Legend has it that around 400 years ago a cyclone whipped up a freak wave that all but destroyed Pukapuka and left only a few survivors: 15 men and two women. The poor women were charged with starting the repopulation of the atoll, and there's been a relaxed attitude to relationships ever since.

Pukapuka has always had a tremendous reputation for *kirikiti* – the name is not a coincidental soundalike, incidentally, it shows how the south Pacific took the game introduced to them by the missionaries over a century ago and adapted it – and many if not most of the great Cook Islands' *kirikiti* players have been either from Pukapuka or descended from Pukapukans.

In the 1920s the American writer Robert Dean Frisbie settled on Pukapuka and wrote about his experiences. In his 1944 book *The Island of Desire* he summed up the place of *kirikiti* in the life of the atoll:

"Presently, in a little clearing, I came upon the 150 people of Leeward Village, playing or watching a studied game of cricket. Two or three men glanced at me in a vaguely preoccupied way, then jerked their heads around to watch the game. Happy-go-lucky old Tapipi, his eyes shifting between me and the players, explained hurriedly that for six hours they had been playing to decide which half of the village should gather coconuts tomorrow for the other half. I then realised that if the British Navy were target-practicing in the offing no one would leave the game. Like children that can play for two hours but cannot work for two minutes, these atoll people can play cricket all day to determine who shall work an hour tomorrow. I mentioned as much to Tapipi. He knitted his brow, pondered my words, and finally opined that it would be hard work gathering coconuts tomorrow, for the people would be stiff and tired from the cricket game."

COSTA RICA

Cricket in Costa Rica, which had its heyday in the first half of the 20th century, is experiencing a modest revival, and a cricket association has been formed to seek Affiliate Membership of the ICC. The game took root in this part of Central America in the late 19th century after Jamaican workers were imported to help build the railway, replacing those of other nationalities who had succumbed to malaria. Many stayed to work in banana plantations or as cocoa planters and, between the two world wars, there were 45 teams in three leagues on the Caribbean coast. Eventually, the West Indian CC was founded by English expats in the capital San José, and in 1986 San José CC itself was revived. The rivalry between San José and Limón – the traditional coastal cricket centre – has continued sporadically. In recent years there have been testimonials for the 80th birthdays of two of Costa Rica's cricket luminaries: Stanford Barton, vice-captain of the Limón team that twice toured Jamaica in the 1930s, and Lance Binns, who scored 30 for a Jamaican Schoolboys XI in 1935-36 against a Yorkshire touring team including Len Hutton. Binns still plays for San José. In August 2000 San José, comprising young masters at the British School and not-so-young resident expats, beat Limón by an innings and 64. *T. R. Illingworth*, **Wisden 2001**

"Whither Costa Rican cricket but for the Second World War?" has not, in truth, ever been a hot topic of debate in the pubs, pavilions and press-boxes of the world, but when you look at the history of the game on the sliver of land joining North and Central America, it's worth dwelling awhile on what might have been. Thanks mainly to its Jamaican population, Costa Rica in the 1930s was a beacon of cricket nestling between the Atlantic and the Pacific. George Headley was a major factor: a folk hero to Jamaicans everywhere, Headley and his West Indies team-mates visited Panama – where he was born while his father was helping to construct the Canal there – and Costa Rica when there was a gap of five weeks between the Third and Fourth Tests on England's 1930 tour of the West Indies. Given that Headley had just scored a hundred in each innings at Georgetown to help West Indies to their first-ever Test victory, it's no surprise that large crowds greeted the banana ship SS *Ariguani* when it docked in both nations with Headley waving cheerily from the deck. He must have been buoyed by the visit – or at least, the generous hospitality appeared to have no adverse after-effects – as he went on to make 223 in the Fourth Test at Sabina Park.

Headley returned in 1933 with Jamaica, who played a game there this time: 4,000 turned out to watch. Regular visits from Caribbean teams throughout the 1930s as well as Caribbean tours by Costa Rican sides helped to keep the momentum going, as well as exposing the local players to a high standard of cricket: the fact that there were 45 clubs in the Limón region alone suggested a bright future lay ahead. Test status was never likely, but there could at least have been a steady supply of good players for the West Indies team – until the war brought things juddering to a halt. Costa Rican cricket would never attain the same heights again.

When the war commenced, Lancelot Binns was working in Jamaica and playing there for one of the leading clubs. Arguably Costa Rica's greatest-ever player, among Binns's many outstanding performances were a knock of 111 against the King's Light Infantry and taking eight for 18 against the British Garrison, including a hat-trick, both before his 18th birthday. Possibly his finest moment came at the age of 15 in February 1936, however, when he was selected for a Jamaican schools team to play the touring Yorkshire county side at Sabina Park. It would have been intimidating enough for any cricketer of the time to come up against a team including Len Hutton, Herbert Sutcliffe, Maurice Leyland and Bill Bowes, let alone a 15-year-old kid working on a banana plantation, but Binns opened the batting and made 30 before playing around a straight one from medium-pacer Tom Smailes. The Jamaicans, who were allowed 15 players, were bowled out for 194 in their first innings before they in turn bowled out the visitors for 222. At the close, Jamaica Schools were 61 for five, with Binns again falling to Smailes, this time for two.

An extraordinary character, Lance Binns kept playing cricket in Costa Rica right up to his death in 2005 at the age of 84, and today the Costa Rican League champions are awarded the Lance Binns Cup in his honour. He'd be delighted to see the progress being made too. Costa Rica became an ICC Affiliate Member in 2002, and the game is growing rapidly among young Costa Ricans: where in 2004 there were only 50 registered junior players, today there are more than 1,000, and that figure continues to rise. If the progress of Costa Rican cricket is any kind of barometer for the likelihood of global war, meanwhile, a look at the precedents suggests it might be time to head for the shelters.

CROATIA

Nepotism is an unlikely formula for the expansion of cricket, not least in a remote outpost in the Adriatic. But the efforts of Dorothy Burrows, an 84-year-old follower of the game on the island of Vis, may yet help the game flourish in Croatia. Burrows, a great-great-niece of the Royal Navy captain Sir William Hoste, succeeded in persuading 28 of Hoste's descendants, some from as far away as Hong Kong, to travel to Vis to play against the cricket club that bears his name. A protégé of Admiral Horatio Nelson, Hoste established a garrison on Vis in 1809 during the Napoleonic Wars, and permitted his men to play cricket as a way of staving off boredom between skirmishes. "We have established a cricket club at this wretched place," he wrote to his mother. "And when we do get anchored for a few hours, it passes away an hour very well." Cricket did not really endure, but a revival towards the end of the 1990s fuelled by expatriate and second-generation Croatian–Australians has led to four cricket clubs springing up in Zagreb, Split and Vis. It took inclusion in the Croatian edition of *Playboy* to arouse cricket in Vis again. The club's co-founder, Rob Dumancic, stumbled across an interview with a local winemaker, Oliver Roki, in which he expressed a vague hope of resuscitating Hoste's sporting legacy. But his interest in the game was far from frivolous. "Apart from one expat and two guys from England, the rest of the team discovered the game seven years ago and had never played it before," said Roki. "We have six or seven kids who can really play, but they have no one to play against." Vis's story stirred the interest of the most famous club of all, MCC, who sent a touring side to face the national team and developmental XIs on Vis's Plisko Polje ground in August. A team boasting former first-class players Darren Bicknell and Rob Turner won all four matches, but they were not cakewalks. Lord's even bought into the spirit of the occasion, appointing Norfolk captain Steve Livermore to skipper MCC (Sir William, born in Ingoldisthorpe, came from the same county). MCC arrived bearing a grant of $US2,500 for the Croatian Cricket Federation, which, along with a donation of $1,250 from the ICC, will be channelled into ECB Level Two coaching courses in the country. A reciprocal visit of the national side to England would seem the next step, but an improvement in results may be required first. Croatia lost all six matches in their ICC European Championship tournament in 2008, and surrendered Division Two status when Israel beat them in a play-off at Zagreb's newly-constructed Budenec Oval ground in October. *James Coyne*, **Wisden 2010**

CUBA

Before Fidel Castro came to power in 1959 there was plenty of cricket in Cuba. Thanks largely to the efforts of Leona Ford, a revival is under way with 19 adult teams including six made up of overseas students. There are also 55 age-group teams. So far, however, there has been no organised inter-club competition; the fact that cricket is only recognised as a recreation and not a sport limits the amount of support it obtains from INDER, the Cuban sports ministry. However, there are hopes of a Cuban national championship in 2005. The best-organised province is the Isle of Youth (Isla de la Juventud) where an INDER employee, Daniel

Garcia, has obtained funding from the provincial government to set up a ground with a pitch based on sand and scoria (solidified lava). Garcia has brought in teams from the local prison (cricket is considered good for self-discipline, I was told), the fire station and a dog club. Apparently the dog club was holding a trial when Daniel and a friend started to play with a kanga cricket set. The dog lovers were smitten and the rest is history. *Gerry Beaton*, **Wisden 2005**

Leona Ford is one of the most remarkable people in world cricket. A retired English professor, she has been the instigator of and driving force behind the resurgence of Cuban cricket over the last decade or so, reviving a sport that had all but died and turning it into a thriving concern. No one person anywhere in the world can have had such an overwhelming and dramatic effect on the development of cricket in their country.

She inherited her passion for cricket from her father, one of the Cuban game's pioneers. Leonard Ford arrived in Cuba from his native Barbados in 1928 to work at the Guantanamo Naval Base. There was quite an influx of Bajan migrant workers to Cuba at the time, many of them seeking employment on the sugar plantations on the east of the island, and many of them cricketers. But Leonard would stand out. An accomplished cricketer back home, he soon became a notable player in his adoptive country; his notability increasing when he founded the Guantanamo Cricket Club within a year of arriving in the country. A passionate promoter of the game, Leonard Ford was at the forefront of every development in cricket in Cuba including, in 1954, playing for the first-ever Cuban national side when they took on a team from Jamaica.

The Cuban Revolution that finally succeeded in 1959 and brought Castro to power saw all sporting institutions nationalised, including cricket clubs. The game of cricket wasn't exactly high on Castro's agenda and – with no official support or sanction – the game all but died with breathtaking speed. One annual match on Emancipation Day in Baragua limped on, but a once-thriving sport that featured a roster of clubs right across Cuba seemed to have been confined to pre-revolutionary history.

Years later, following the death of her father, Leonora Ford began undertaking research into her family history and soon noticed something. Throughout her childhood cricket had been practically another member of the family. The walls of their Guantanamo home were covered with photographs of cricketers and there were always meetings of cricket administrators taking place in the house, which was situated just an underarm lob from the Guantanamo cricket ground itself. Weekends were spent either playing or watching the game. But when Leonora began exploring the national archives, she realised there was barely a word written about cricket. Not only had the game died out, there was very little to suggest it had actually existed in the first place.

She decided to write a book on the history of Cuban cricket so there would be a tangible record of it even if the game itself was a mere memory. In addition she resolved to at least attempt a Cuban cricket revival, even if it just meant getting a few kids playing in the street.

In 1998 Ford presented a paper about Cuba's cricket legacy and her desire to revive it to the West Indian Welfare Association at their annual general meeting. Her passion and enthusiasm won over the room, but her words interested one man in particular. Sir Howard Cooke, the governor of Jamaica, was a cricket man. Not only that, he'd also played for that first Jamaican side that had toured Cuba, and hence he'd met and played against Leonora's father. It was a tremendous coincidence; the catalyst to launch Cuba back into the cricketing sphere. Cooke had some cricket equipment sent over and enlisted the help of a friend of his, Courtney Walsh, to promote the game in Cuba. The Cuban Cricket Commission was formed with Leonora at its head. A sports journalist from Trinidad organised some coaching. And when the Cuban sports ministry officially recognised the sport in 2001 the outlook was rosy.

The recognition came with a caveat, however: while cricket was approved, it was approved merely as a recreational activity rather than an officially sanctioned sport, which meant no funding. Cuban cricket would have to look elsewhere for financial support to power the comeback. Yet, thanks to generous donations and a tie-up with UK Sport, within four years of Leonora's speech to WIWA there were more than 1,000 Cuban children receiving cricket coaching and eight senior teams had begun playing regularly. Perhaps most fittingly cricket returned to Guantanamo in 2001, when a Guantanamo team took on a Havana side at a small football stadium. Guantanamo won by four wickets. If Leona needed confirmation that she was honouring her father's legacy, that was it.

Affiliation to the ICC followed in 2002, and in 2006 – when Castro instigated a policy of looking towards the Caribbean to halt the progress of the cultural Americanisation of Cuban youth – he decided he approved of cricket after all. There is a story that Castro even tried cricket once, on a state visit to Barbados. Seeing a match taking place as he drove past, he stopped the car, asked what was going on, and marched on to the field and demanded to have a go with the bat. With baseball being the most popular sport in the country it was no surprise that Castro held the bat like he was at Yankee Stadium. Once at the wicket he insisted that his host bowl at him and hence it was that two teams of Bajan cricketers saw play suspended in order that the president of Barbados might bowl at Fidel Castro who, reports said, had a whale of a time.

In 2007 came a chance to shine on the international stage when the Cuban national side was invited to participate in the 2008 Stanford Series, one of the Twenty20 tournaments organised by the soon-to-be-disgraced American billionaire Allen Stanford. However, America's policy of non-recognition when it comes to Cuba also prohibits American citizens fraternising with Cubans without permission. Hence, shortly before the tournament, Cuba's invitation had to be withdrawn.

Despite this, the progress of cricket in Cuba under the guidance of Leonora Ford remains constant, encouraging and indefatigably Cuban.

In 1895 a young journalist named Winston Churchill visited Cuba. He noted how Britain had briefly taken control of the island towards the end of the 18th century and grew all misty-eyed at the missed opportunity for a "free and prosperous" British colony that "sent its ponies to Hurlingham and its cricketers to Lord's".

Instead, who knows, with the astounding potential of the game in Cuba and the unquenchable drive of its patron, maybe one day we'll see England sending its cricketers to Ford's instead.

CZECH REPUBLIC

Cricket in the Czech Republic enjoyed another year of progress, even if most Czechs remained oblivious of its attractions. Prague CC, formed in 1997, were joined by Olomouc, and there is a chance of a third club, at Ostrava. Several cities, including Prague and Olomouc, offer coaching in some schools, and around some 600 Czech children have now played cricket. Adults, meanwhile, can sign up for twice-weekly summer net sessions in the capital, and an indoor league may follow in 2003. Prague CC enjoyed a busy season, reaching the final of the Golden Duck tournament in Lodi, Italy, and doing well – four wins, three losses and a draw – in various friendlies against Munich International, Cricketers Anonymous, Berlin, and the Dutch side Haarlem Wolves in a two-day game. Prague welcomed teams from Olomouc and Bratislava, another new club over the border in Slovakia, and won both. Two young Czechs who discovered cricket in 2002 went on to notable achievements. Lukas Fencl, a convert from softball, adjusted so well that he scored the first century by a Czech cricketer, while Magda Pokludova, who went to Bath on a student exchange, was representing Somerset in the Women's County Championship by August. The next challenge is to find a Czech-speaking full-time development officer. *Tony Brennan*, **Wisden 2003**

Magda Pokludova played seven matches for Somerset. She batted only twice, making 14 runs, and bowled two overs. Unspectacular figures they may seem in black and white, but they hide meteoric progress. "On June 12, 2000, I saw a game of cricket for the first time in my life," she said. Pokludova was instantly hooked, and when she sought to continue her studies abroad the possibility of playing cricket contributed significantly to her plumping for the UK. Almost exactly two years after catching sight of cricket for the first time, Magda Pokludova was stepping out on to the field at Kimbolton School in Huntingdonshire as a Somerset county player to face Lancashire.

"Now I play for Prague, Somerset and other teams in Bath," she said, "with cricketers of all ages and both sexes."

EAST TIMOR

Sandwiched between the beach and mountains, around three kilometres from downtown Dili, is a small dirt road where, once a month, cricket is played by a motley collection of expatriates, mainly Australian, and East Timorese. Play gets stopped by stray goats, pigs, children meandering across the "pitch" on the salt plain, and occasionally by people learning to drive. Sometimes the children chasing the ball take off with it – when a child stops the ball, it's an automatic four. Kit was an issue (the bamboo stumps kept breaking) until we managed to acquire two large bags of cricket gear in return for 500kg of rice. Everyone was happy. Numbers vary and we have played six-a-side up to 21-a-side, especially during the period of reconstruction after post-independence violence, which brought an influx of Australians. In 2001 we played in the Bali Sixes, the organisers provocatively pitting us against the country's former rulers Indonesia in our first game. We hope to return this year, seeking revenge. The team has four East Timorese regulars, who are athletic fielders and deadly in throwing down a set of stumps. But our games are highly social, and the few Portuguese and Americans who turn up are allowed to chuck. *Jim Richards*, **Wisden 2004**

EL SALVADOR

Cricket in El Salvador can trace its roots back to an email from an Englishman about to end his stint teaching at the British School: "Have regional cricket contacts & barely used cricket set. Anyone interested?" Drawing inspiration both from this and from another cricketing expat who had once represented the Colombian national team, a resident Zimbabwean took up the baton, even if the hot Salvadorian summer caused one local schoolboy to faint – and prompted a rethink: Twenty20, which allows players to return home for some much-needed lunchtime shade, is now the dominant format. Conditions remain variable: flat land in this mountainous country is scarce, so the cricket played is on a borrowed football field, with the pitch mowed on Saturday mornings. Predictably the bounce is lively: helmets are a must for the younger players. Our three teams are slowly getting stronger as curious locals join in – some stay, some go – and interested players are guaranteed a game. The national side has always contained at least six Salvadorians, even if first efforts look more like baseball and bent-arm bowling is viewed initially as the cricketing equivalent of a dive in football: cheating, but worth a try. The Easter Cup tournament – largely funded by a Sri Lankan businessman – received good press coverage. Now we just need better facilities. *Andrew Murgatroyd,* **Wisden 2008**

ESTONIA

Like most good ideas and institutions, the Estonian Cricket Club (*Esti Kriketi Klubi*) was born in a pub, in this case The Lost Continent in Tallinn. The first club email from the chairman, Kristian Garancis, said, "Practice will be on Sunday 1300hrs providing no snow." That was 1998, and from there we developed. The first pitch was an outdoor basketball court, with one old bat and a tennis ball. We progressed to a very bumpy soccer pitch in a lovely setting surrounded by forest (and topless lady sunbathers), but under threat from scheduled soccer matches. Later that same year the club moved on to the Hippodroom, the trotting track, where the management have been excellent hosts – and most flexible, as we built an all-weather pitch in the middle of the racecourse. The European Cricket Council have been most helpful and provided two start-up cricket kits. EKK facilities are now excellent, with three bars and the best wicket in the region. There are 30 regular players from nine nations, including Estonia. We have played home fixtures against Helsinki, Riga and Stockholm, and have started a programme to develop cricket in Estonian schools. Touring sides are welcome: Tallinn is a wonderful old Hanseatic city and an excellent place to visit. *Philip Marsdale*, **Wisden 2001**

It's fair to say that Estonian cricket has had a bit of a decade since this entry. Inspired by Estonian businessman Garancis, who'd seen the 1996 Boxing Day Test between Australia and the West Indies with friends in Melbourne and returned determined to bring the game to the Baltic – first stop, his favourite Indian restaurant in Tallinn – the game has flourished to a degree unthinkable during those pioneering forays on to a basketball court smacking a tennis ball about.

By 2004 an Estonian Cricket Board had been formed, and three years later there was enough interest to form a league of four teams playing in a round-robin format. The expansion of the budget-airline boom into the Baltics around the same time brought so many touring teams from Britain that the Estonians found themselves fulfilling up to 60 fixtures a season. All that practice soon paid off: in 2008 a fledgling national team travelled to a European Twenty20 tournament in north Wales and came back as winners. Such was the interest back home that the team were greeted at the airport by a crew from Estonian national television.

This rapid improvement raised approving eyebrows at the ICC, and Estonia was granted Affiliate status. The funding this engendered allowed the game to be encouraged at junior levels through an impressive schools' development programme. Cricket had become much less an activity for expats looking for a taste of home and more a game that Estonians took to on their own terms.

In 2012 Estonia hosted Division Three of the Euro Twenty20 tournament. With the Tallinn crowd boosted by the unlikely attendance of Shane Warne and Elizabeth Hurley, Estonia emerged as victors and progressed to the Division Two tournament in Corfu. While they couldn't repeat their success at the higher level, wins over Malta and Luxembourg demonstrated that they could certainly hold their own.

Estonian cricket is one of the world game's current success stories, to the extent that these days they don't have to tempt potential visiting teams merely with the promise of a stroll around "a wonderful old Hanseatic city", or even "topless lady sunbathers".

Well, OK, maybe topless lady sunbathers.

ETHIOPIA

Cricket used to be played regularly in Addis Ababa at the General Wingate School, with British and Indian teachers. A 1967 guidebook advised cricket lovers simply to turn up at the school on Saturday mornings if they wanted a game. However, these teachers left during the rule of General Mengistu, and we are left with only a few scratch games involving staff, students and parents from the Sandford English Community School. They are played on the football field, which is composed of volcanic rock with a covering of soil and grass. The pitch is marked out by string, then the groundsman cuts it with his sickle, and the clippings are taken away in a sack to feed his donkey. The bigger rocks are pulled out by hand, but it is still imperative to use a soft ball. Few Ethiopians play, although we can always find some students to join in, and there is talent among the batsmen. We also had a wonderful fast bowler here, a young man from Sierra Leone called Sahr Komba, but he has now gone to an American university and plays basketball. *Stephen Spawls,* **Wisden 1997**

Other than Bert Oldfield's visit to Ethiopia in the 1960s (see introduction), Ethiopia is a barren nation when it comes to cricket. Matches were played regularly at the Wingate School, even after Mengistu came to power in 1974, but otherwise the nation's cricket heritage is minimal. Haile Selassie attended part of the India v Pakistan Test while visiting Bombay in 1952 – so he at least had something to talk to Bert Oldfield about when he rolled up more than a decade later – and Ethiopia did have one fairly decent cricketer in John Asfaw, who played for Rugby School against Marlborough at Lord's in 1959, but … well, that's about it.

There is one tiny Ethiopian cricket outpost, however. The town of Shashamane, 150 miles south of the capital Addis Ababa, is home to a community of around 200 Rastafarians. In the 1960s Haile Selassie invited Rastas to come "home" to Ethiopia, assigning them 500 acres of land in Shashamane, and an eager clutch made the journey. But what they discovered when they arrived was far from the Promised Land: resented by much of the local populace, they found work and income hard to come by.

Even today the community is small and practically stateless: not eligible for citizenship and still regarded as unwelcome outsiders by the Ethiopian population who had previously occupied the area, the Rastafarian community has a twilight status, neither one thing nor the other. They spend their days working as handymen and artists or selling souvenirs to tourists, and playing cricket. Despite having only basic equipment donated by the British Embassy, the cricketers of Shashamane practise twice a week and in 2012 played their first proper game, losing to the Embassy by 35 runs in Addis Ababa. They are hoping for a return match and to arrange fixtures against some of the other embassies in Addis.

As for the 6ft 4ins erstwhile quickie Shahr Komba, it seems he was never tempted back to the cricket field. In 2011 he was playing basketball in England, for the Hemel Hempstead Storm.

FALKLAND ISLANDS

The annual match between the Governor's XI and the Forces resulted in a thrilling one-run win for the Governor's XI, reducing the Forces' lead in the series to 4–3. The contest is played on the world's southernmost cricket field, Mount Pleasant Oval, for a handsome trophy, mounted on rock, representing a penguin's beak emerging from an egg. The Oval can hold the entire population of the Falkland Islands: 4,000. The matting wicket traditionally favours bowlers, but only when they have the wind behind them. Those bowling into the wind regularly struggle to reach the opposite end. *Richard Heller*, **Wisden 1999**

FINLAND

Success for the national side at the ECC Representative Festival in Zagreb in 2002 – they beat Croatia and Slovenia – was a welcome reward for Finnish Cricket Association officials who had worked hard to give cricket healthy roots. Helsinki CC was formed in 1974 but cricket was slow to establish itself. It expanded in the mid-1990s, and the creation of the FCA, together with help from the European Cricket Council, has increased participation so that around one-fifth of the country's 350 cricketers are Finnish citizens.

Helsinki CC won the eight-team league from the champions SKK, while the newly formed Espoo CC ended an encouraging third. Another new side, the Finnish Naval Academy CC, joined MTS as the second team not made up of expats. Meanwhile, women's friendlies were played between SKK of Helsinki, Tampere CC and Guttsta of Sweden. A "Spirit of Cricket" weekend was held in May, and in July, more than 20 teams from Finland, Britain, Estonia and Finland battled for the SKK Cricket Sixes. The elements continue to make cricket in Finland a singular experience: a while back, play was stopped when an elk galloped out of the woods, and early in the 2002 season bowlers ran over snow on their run-ups. *Andy Armitage*, **Wisden 2004**

When Andrew Armitage relocated to Finland in 1988 he feared that his cricket career, hitherto played out on club grounds around Manchester, was among the collateral damage of emigration: of all the nations in the world fewer seemed likely to be a hotbed of the summer game than Finland. A quarter of a century on, however, Armitage finds himself the president of the Finnish Cricket Association, overseeing a sport growing rapidly in popularity among both expats and Finns. And it's largely thanks to a chance encounter in a park.

"One day a little while after I'd arrived in Finland I stumbled across a group of people knocking around in one of the central parks of Helsinki and couldn't believe my eyes," he recalls. "These guys turned out to be members of the only cricket club in the country at the time, Helsinki CC, who played their cricket either abroad or with teams from the embassies. Seeing them, I was suitably inspired to do something about making cricket a reality in Finland."

The word spread among expats, and ad hoc games would take place until, in the mid-1990s, participation reached a level that meant new clubs were formed. Armitage helped to found the Stadin Kriketti Kerho, the City Cricket Club, and was instrumental in the 1999 foundation of the Finnish Cricket Association. A year later, as

Finland earned ICC Affiliate status, he became president, a post he has held ever since.

For all the sterling work he's done for Finnish cricket over the years however, the most awe-inspiring thing about Andrew Armitage is, for me, the fact he was on the field for the only recorded instance in cricket history of "elk stopped play". When a giant, snorting half-ton antlered male thundered across the field during a Finnish league fixture, Andrew Armitage was there.

"I was fielding in the covers in an SKK game at the central park ground of Ruskeasuo," he recalls. "It's a ground with horse stables around half the boundary and open park and forest around the rest, but only a stone's throw away from Helsinki's main street."

Not exactly the kind of cricket location that would have you thinking, "Hmm, better keep half an eye out for elk," even in Finland. But sure enough, after some brief rustling from the undergrowth, out of the trees and onto the field burst a full-grown, honking elk.

"As you can imagine, having only previously seen pictures of elks on warning signs at the sides of roads, to come face to face with a male elk about twice the size of a horse while chasing down a cover-drive was something of a shock," says Armitage, with a cricketer's gift for understatement. "The elk did not appear to be really interested in cricket: it did an about-turn and headed off back into the forest."

The players, however, remained stoic in the face of such mammalian cricketing drama. Well, possibly. "Play was not stopped for longer than an extended toilet break," says Armitage.

Notwithstanding cameos from agitated *alces alces*, Finnish cricket continues to go from strength to strength, with the progress charted in that *Wisden 2004* entry gaining momentum with each passing year. The FCA now has 23 member clubs from Helsinki in the south to Oulu, 500km to the north and nudging the Arctic Circle, and the game is even taking root beyond the expat community.

"Finns are generally a sport-crazy people interested in giving everything a try," says Armitage, "and we have found that after overcoming the initial reservations associated with playing a sport in white clothes that has far too many rules and can end in a draw after five days, they tend to take to the game fairly easily. School sports have traditionally been strong in Finland, so the majority of children do tend to have reasonable hand–eye co-ordination and can hit the ball well. Bowling, however, is a more difficult proposition, though we have for many years co-operated with the elite performance training centre 'Kuortane', where many of Finland's javelin heroes have honed their skills, in the hope that we can convert a few of them to 90mph fast bowlers ..."

The momentum should be maintained with the construction of Finland's first purpose-built cricket venue: the National Cricket Ground in the town of Kerava in the far south of the country.

"This will, we feel, be both the base block for building the game in future as well as the catalyst behind driving forward the indigenous population's awareness of cricket," says Armitage. "Promotion of the Kerava NCG to the local Finnish corporate community will open new doors for Cricket Finland to generate much-needed extra funding, enabling us to drive better-quality coaching forward in delivering a more widespread participation programme in schools."

The picturesque, tree-fringed ground at Kerava is in an important location for Finns: Sibelius wrote most of the magnificent national symphonic poem *Finlandia* in the town. Cricket may never earn a similar place at the forefront of Finnish identity, but with its own ground, increased participation and the dedication of people like Andrew Armitage, the future of Finnish cricket may be hinted at in Sibelius's early name for *Finlandia*: *Suomi Herää* – Finland awakens.

FRANCE

France retained the Nations Cup at Zuoz, Switzerland, in astonishing circumstances. They beat Germany by one run in a pulsating 50-over final. The unwitting hero was France's last man, David Bordes, who was hit on the forehead, and staggered through for a single at the end of the French innings before collapsing with a fractured skull. With two balls left, Germany, chasing 267, were 260 for nine: a top-edge fumbled by third man plopped over the rope for six. The Germans completed the two runs they needed for victory while the last ball was still skying to mid-on, where Valentin Brumant eventually caught it. So the Bordes head-bye proved a match-winner. He had to spend the next two weeks in hospital, and was ill for some time, but, happily, was able to resume playing indoor cricket before Christmas. Bordes normally bats with a helmet but did not bother this time because he had only the one ball to face. In a group game against Switzerland, Germany scored 467 for one in their 50 overs, including an unbroken stand of 349 between Shamaz Khan, a Pakistani-born naturalised German, and Abdul Bhatti. Shamaz scored 200 not out and Bhatti 179 not out. *Simon Hewitt and Brian Fell,* **Wisden 1998**

MCC marked London 2012 by crossing the Channel in June for an Olympic commemoration fixture. It was conceived as a rematch of sorts of the 1900 Paris Olympics, when Devon County Wanderers, representing Great Britain, beat the Union des Sociétés Françaises de Sports Athlétiques (France) by 158 runs in a two-innings game (see *Wisden 2012*, page 108). This time, a Twenty20 game was played at the charming Château de Thoiry, west of Paris. To a soundtrack of roaring lions and other exotic wildlife from the zoo in the grounds, MCC won by 34 runs. That was a far cry from the last time they were in town: in 1989, to mark the bicentenary of the

French Revolution, they slipped to a seven-wicket defeat against a France team led by an Irishman, Jack Short, and containing just one Frenchman. It was a hollow victory – cricket hasn't progressed much since, and remains largely the preserve of expats. But that may change. The France Cricket Association has invested heavily in Kwik Cricket, introducing the game into 150 schools in September. The aim is to reach 300 to 500 schools – and 40,000 children – within three years. Around 150 teachers have been trained up in the basics of the game; that figure is expected to reach 800. A full-time project co-ordinator has been hired, along with five regional development officers. The FCA have also forged an Anglo-French relationship with Kent: 18-year-old leg-spinner Zika Ali has spent time at the Academy in Canterbury, and received a leg-spin masterclass from board patron Richie Benaud at Thoiry. If the kids come through, then in 15 years perhaps MCC will be able to play a team of thoroughbred Frenchmen. *Barney Spender*, **Wisden 2013**

It's a vista as English as buttered crumpets: the white-clad figures on the green, the smattering of spectators in deckchairs, the whirling of the bowler's arms, the swish of the bat, the thwack of ball into the wicket-keeper's gloves and the mass appeal from the fielders of, erm, "*Eh alors!*"

For this is not a village green nestling among the Sussex Downs or Yorkshire Dales but a scene that is found in an increasing number of towns and villages across that most unlikely of cricketing strongholds: France.

With 1,200 registered players, more than 60 clubs with their own grounds, and government plans to introduce cricket to those 500 schools across France in the next few years, these are exciting times for French cricketers. Yet France has always had an extraordinary cricketing legacy; one dating back to the dawn of the game itself.

A 15th-century document turned up recently detailing a riot that took place over a game of "*criquet*" at St Omer in the Pas de Calais in 1478. It's led to speculation that the most English of games may actually have originated in France which, in terms of felling an iron horse of national pride, would be a little like unearthing de Gaulle's birth certificate and finding he was born in Tooting.

France's defeat in the 1900 Olympics also means that to this day they hold the only Olympic silver medal ever awarded for cricket: the Paris Games were the only Olympics ever to feature the sport, and only France and a team billed as England actually turned up (the French team mainly comprised players from the Standard Athletic Club, formed ten years earlier by English labourers working on the construction of the Eiffel Tower, while the Devon side just happened to be in town on tour). Neither team knew they'd contested an Olympic final until after the event: they'd just thought the brouhaha surrounding the game was because it was a part of the Paris Exposition.

Like most Anglo-French encounters, cricket matches involving the two nations have always, it seems, had an aspect of the unusual. When the MCC was in its infancy the first overseas tour was to be a jaunt across the Channel. Unfortunately, it being 1789, the tour became an unsung and forgotten victim of the French Revolution. The players arrived in France, only to have to beat a pretty hasty retreat when they realised what was going on. Two hundred years later MCC finally fulfilled their revolution-stopped-play fixture by taking on a French national team. Any knitting descendants of Madame Desfarge who happened to be on the boundary would have seen France beat the most famous cricket club in the world, captained by former Surrey skipper Roger Knight, by six wickets, with an Irishman, Jack Short, making a match-winning 73 not out.

In terms of excitement the game against Germany in which David Bordes' painful head-bye proved decisive will take some beating. It was such an extraordinary game that it made *Wisden's* own list of the 100 most memorable games of the 20th century, but Bordes didn't simply disappear into the wispy caverns of cricket history: these days he coaches the French national side and is the Technical Advisor to France Cricket.

Given the rapid development of the game in France, there could well be more thrilling games to come, although hopefully involving fewer cracked skulls. Either way, the story of cricket in France is one that translates as well as the French phrase for a wicket maiden – *vierge couronnée*, literally a "crowned virgin".

GERMANY

It came as a great relief to the cricket community when the Berlin Olympic Stadium authorities reversed their decision to evict cricket from the last surviving ground in the capital. The game has been played at Körnerplatz, inside the Olympic Park, for 60 years, so Berlin's cricketers were shocked when they turned up for the new season to discover the artificial mat and base had been pulled up, and the practice nets removed. The reason was that age-old worldwide cricket problem: flying cricket balls. The authorities were concerned that unwitting passers-by were at risk of being hit, and might press the city for compensation. A local and international media campaign, which included a Facebook group and sympathetic articles in *The Times* and *Daily Telegraph*, helped bring the two parties around the table. Happily, the mat was relaid and the cricketers returned. The dialogue has continued, and it looks like cricket will survive. Not only that, the authorities are considering making two pitches available for 2012 – the second directly behind the stadium on Maifeld, the vast lawn often used for polo and, in a different era, for Nazi Party rallies on May Day. Last season DSSC Berlin, one of ten teams in the capital, won the 50-over Championship for the seventh time. The past few years have witnessed a remarkable growth in clubs all across Germany: there are now over 70 affiliated to the German Cricket Federation, and six more on the horizon. Cricket is played to some degree in all 16 federated states, and an increasing number of schools and universities are taking to the sport. *Brian Fell,* **Wisden 2012**

HONG KONG

As the handover of control from Britain to China grew ever closer, cricket in Hong Kong changed too. While the traditional centres, Kowloon Cricket Club and Hong Kong Cricket Club, with their magnificent facilities, continued to play a major role, a growing number of ethnic Asian players joined in. In particular, junior cricket has taken off, and hundreds of young Chinese players have been introduced to the game. The Hong Kong Sixes, the colony's most famous event, moved from the Kowloon club to the huge Hong Kong stadium in 1996. This caused much debate and the event lost some of its old flavour; but the move had to be made if the event was to grow in international stature. It was a big success, despite the effects of Typhoon Willy on the first day, and West Indies beat India in the final. We can now look forward to further big matches in the territory and, as a result of the interest shown in trips to China and Japan by Hong Kong coaches, growth throughout the region. We can foresee the day when the Hong Kong team is made up of Chinese cricketers, and China is a serious player within the game. *Russell Mawhinney,* **Wisden 1997**

HUNGARY

A contender for the most ambitious international cricket venue conceived in 2011 was the St George's Oval, carved out of a disused Hungarian quarry. Surrounded on three sides by cliffs and on the fourth by tiered flowerbeds made from old tyres, it promises stunning elevated views and a unique clifftop spectator experience. St George's also claims to be the world's first eco venue, made exclusively out of natural or recycled materials and operating on solar power. The quarry, in Iszkaszentgyorgy, 80km south-west of Budapest, was purchased in June and transformed into a cricket ground in six months by a passionate group of volunteers headed by an Englishman, Andy Grieve. The plan is to complete the development this year with a grass square and a clubhouse. St George's should be as busy as any ground in a Test nation, with a packed schedule ranging from the local league fixtures to international tournaments. Its principal function will be as the base for the Hungarian Cricket Association's ambitious development programme, with cricket workshops held in a local castle. This should help Hungary's drive for ICC Affiliate status. The national team did their cause no harm in 2011 by successfully defending the Euro Twenty20 title, on home soil at Szodiglet, the biggest ground in Central and Eastern Europe. *Tim Brooks*, **Wisden 2012**

Alas, the extraordinary story of St George's Oval didn't have a happy ending, at least not in cricket terms. "Unfortunately the other investor pulled out," Andy Grieve told me, "and now I am using the land for golf and vegetables."

Despite this setback, Hungarian cricket continues to make great progress. The game has only been going in organised form since 2007 and a meeting instigated by Grieve in a Budapest Irish theme pub (appropriately named after the Nobel prize-winning author and first-class cricketer Samuel Beckett). The Hungarian Cricket Association was formed, a league comprising six teams established, and by 2010 cricket in Hungary had progressed as far as the national side winning the Euro Twenty20 tournament in Skopje, Macedonia. They beat Russia by three wickets in the final with a ball to spare after Sufiyan Mohammed anchored the total with a brisk 82, including five sixes in one over, and thrashed the 17 runs required from the final over from five balls in gathering darkness. Hungary retained their title the following year at their brand new Szodiglet Oval ground outside Budapest.

This is no mere expat plaything, however: there has been a concerted effort to introduce the game to Hungary's Roma community in an effort to promote the mixing of communities, while in the city of Debrecen a group of Afghans has set up their own team. Sadly, they won't be playing at St George's Oval anytime soon unless they bring their golf clubs. Hungary's own Field of Dreams may not have materialised but, with ICC Affiliate Member status achieved in 2012 and participation among all sorts of Hungarian communities on the rise, it's a setback the game there can probably take on the chin.

ICELAND

The most northerly and most remarkable of cricketing nations arrived on the scene in 2000, not, in the normal fashion, through the efforts of exiles, but owing to the extraordinary vision of a handful of Icelanders. The story of Icelandic cricket began at the University of Iceland a few years ago when some students caught a glimpse of the game on Sky News. "Everyone was dressed in white," said one of them, Ragnar Kristinsson, "with pressed trousers, and we wanted to do the same." But none of the TV channels in Iceland showed more than snatches of this mysterious game. However, in 1999, Kristinsson was on holiday in Cyprus during the great World Cup semi-final between Australia and South Africa, and was entranced again. The following Sunday he and a friend were in London and decided they had to be near Lord's for the final. Outside, they met some Pakistanis, leaving in disgust as their team hurtled to defeat, who readily handed over their tickets. Kristinsson was now firmly hooked. He wrote to the European Cricket Council, who sent a set of starter equipment, and a couple of teams emerged: Kylfan (Icelandic for "the bat") in Reykjavik and Ungmennafelagid Glaumur in Stykkisholmer (believed to be the world's most northerly club, as well as the most unpronounceable). The teams mostly comprised native Icelanders, with coaching from some better-informed expats. Iceland's entry into international cricket came in 2000, when Manchester barrister and aspirant Liberal Democrat politician, Jonathan Rule, decided this was the perfect venue for his stag night. He assembled a group of friends in a beautiful valley outside Reykjavik to take on the locals. With the help of the émigrés, the Icelanders scored 107 on a bumpy football pitch. The visitors (said to be swaying slightly at the crease after the previous evening's entertainment) lurched to 94 in fading light, watched by rather more journalists and cameras than their cricket usually justifies. The headline "Iceland beats England at cricket" appeared in the following morning's paper. **Wisden 2001**

While Iceland is certainly one of the most recent converts to cricket – and converted by television and locals rather than expats too – the games mentioned in this entry aren't the first to have taken place there. *Wisden 1944*, for example, tells of two matches played in a Reykjavik football stadium between the RAF and the Royal Navy the previous year, both won by the airmen, by 36 and 24 runs respectively.

In fact it's possible there was an unlikely but rather nice literary angle to this pair of wartime matches. Serving in the RAF in Iceland at that time was a man with a contender for the most English name ever bestowed over a font: Cecil Wigglesworth. He had played for the RAF at first-class level in a six-wicket victory over the Army at The Oval in 1927, and also featured in a drawn game at Lord's against the Royal Navy two years later. In 1930 he even turned out for Straits Settlement against the Federated Malay States in Kuala Lumpur. The chances are that, given his decent cricketing pedigree and presence in Reykjavik on RAF duties at the time, Wigglesworth would have been in the side for the two games against the Navy. The literary connection here is that Wigglesworth is widely believed to have been the inspiration for Biggles. But there's more. Also serving in the RAF in Iceland at that time was another man with a frankly splendid name, John Battersby Crompton Lamburn, the younger brother of Richmal Crompton and the boy on whom the *Just William* stories are based. This means that, quite deliciously, two of the most enduring characters in British literature may have been on the same cricket team trying to read the unpredictable bounce from a bumpy football field in Reykjavik in August 1943. I can't say it definitely happened, but there's a pretty good chance that these two men were on the field together: they certainly knew each other. The thought of Biggles calling Just William for a quick single is a pleasing one wherever it might have happened, let alone in the shadow of Icelandic volcanoes among wing-commanders and rear-admirals.

There are some that claim a form of cricket was being played in Iceland rather further back than that. The Icelandic Vikings used to play a game called *knattleikr* that some cricket historians claim is a medieval ancestor of cricket. At this historical distance it's hard to give a detailed analysis of the game for comparison, but *knattleikr* appears in at least five of the Icelandic sagas. The cricket connection seems to be that a hard ball was hit with a stick and that the games could sometimes last for several days, but otherwise on the face of it *knattleikr* seems to have more in common with hockey or lacrosse than cricket.

One major proponent of the *knattleikr* theory was the Copenhagen-based co-author of *The Story of Continental Cricket* Peter S. Hargreaves, who contributed Danish cricket news to *Wisden* as well as submitting Cricket Round the World items for many years. His *Wisden* obituary in 2011 noted how "*Wisden* editors who were less convinced of Danish cricket's vital global importance than he was, or who rendered Danish orthography incorrectly, were rewarded by long, closely typed letters of complaint."

Yet for all these historical precedents, from the literary to the Norse, it's pretty certain that the first game of what we know as cricket in Iceland actually involving Icelanders was between Reykjavik's Kylfan club and Ungmennafelagid Glaumur from Stykkisholmer in 2000. Ungmennafelagid Glaumur – who claim to be the northernmost club in the world and whose name translates a little anticlimactically as Glaumur Youth Club – won the game, and when newspaper reports appeared in the following days it alerted expats in Iceland from England, India and Pakistan that there was some cricket happening up there in the North Atlantic. Additional clubs were formed, experienced players were able to help the Icelandic novices, and a healthy culture of cricket soon developed.

Probably the peak of Icelandic cricket to date came in 2003, when a team from a British bank who called themselves the Effigies briefly toured the country with Henry Blofeld in tow, flying there in an aeroplane piloted by Bruce Dickinson from Iron Maiden. On their whistle-stop tour the Effigies played a match under the midnight sun and another on a snow-covered glacier accessible only by snowmobile. Nothing in Icelandic cricket will ever, it seems, be remotely conventional.

In 2011 the tremendous Fellowship of Fairly Odd Places Cricket Club – a team of veterans from the Netherlands whose fixture list features matches that take place in, well, you know – arrived in Iceland. In the past FOFOP CC have played a match against the Vatican in Rome and played a game in two countries at once on a field that straddled the Dutch-Belgian border. On this occasion they had the honour of being the first team to be defeated by an Icelandic national side. They did have one consolation, though: bowler Robert Kottman's hat-trick is believed to be the northernmost ever taken in the world.

INDONESIA

In 2000, Indonesia, the world's fourth-most populous country with more than 200 million inhabitants, had about ten indigenous cricketers. Now the figure is around 8,000, and in 2005 a national Under-15 team took part in the first East Asia Pacific tournament, beating Fiji, Tonga, Samoa and Japan. This growth had significant help from ICC, who helped upgrade the administration, train coaches and target primary schools for development. The most unusual event in the calendar is the Bajo Cricket 20s, held near the Komodo National Park in Flores. Through the energy of one Indonesian, Laurence Johani, the game has entered a whole new area. In the Bajo 20s players walk barefoot through the bush to play on a mud wicket carved out of a buffalo paddock. Foreign players can enjoy a raw and joyful form of cricket, go to watch Komodo dragons and dive on pristine biodiverse coral reefs. *Alan Wilson*, **Wisden 2006**

IRAN

Over the past two years, cricket has begun thriving among migrant workers from the subcontinent and there are 12 local teams. A cricket ground has been built at the Azadi Stadium in Teheran with a capacity of 5,000. Teams from Sharjah and Baluchistan have visited. A national coach, Hossain Ali Salimian from Karachi University, has been appointed, and the Baseball Federation of the Islamic Republic of Iran, which also covers cricket, is keen to affiliate to ICC. The British are not playing a role in this: the small diplomatic staff in Teheran did not contain any cricketers in 1994, and the city's British community now comprises one resident businessman. **Wisden 1995**

Cricket in Iran has come a long way since this rather enigmatic Cricket Round the World entry. Indeed the situation in the country today is almost the opposite to that described above. Over the past two decades the focus of Iranian cricket has shifted away from migrant workers and Teheran almost entirely to Iranians at the other end of the country.

It's fair to say of most of the countries featured in Cricket Round the World that the game thrives in the capital cities if it thrives at all and, certainly in recent years, the impetus has come mainly from migrant workers and students from the subcontinent. Iran turns that situation completely on its head.

It sounds strange to say that cricket is flourishing in a country of 78 million people that has only four dedicated cricket grounds, but cricket in Iran is not about facilities or numbers, it's about spirit; about playing for the love of the game whenever and wherever you can.

In fact, you'd be hard pressed to find more dedicated and determined cricketers anywhere in the world than those from Nikshahr in the far south-east of the country. A thousand miles from Teheran, Nikshahr is in a mountainous part of Baluchistan roughly 100 miles from the Pakistani border. Cricket and mountains don't usually make effective bedfellows, and in Baluchistan the terrain means that the players have to walk for two hours, often rising before dawn, to reach their nearest vaguely cricket-friendly location. This would be remarkable enough in itself if their destination was a well-kept grass outfield surrounding a pitch of even bounce, or even a matting wicket that produced the occasional snorter whizzing past the nose off a good length, but no, what greets the Nikshahr cricketers is a dusty, grey expanse strewn with rocks and rubble on which someone long ago laid a bumpy strip of concrete that does for a pitch. Temperatures can reach 45°C and, until a couple of years ago when an impressed businessman provided a shelter, there was no shade to be found. If that wasn't hard enough, the cricketers also have to carry their own drinking water in coolers on their trek, meaning that it has to be fairly strictly rationed. Despite these hardships, not to mention the shabby state of their equipment, the cricketers of Nikshahr stay and play all day before packing up and making the return journey on foot as the sun sets behind the mountains.

As dedication among amateur cricketers goes, it certainly beats managing to put off lunch with the in-laws in order to make a club game. It's no wonder that Iqbal Sikander, the Asian Cricket Council's development officer for Iran, seems permanently wide-eyed as he travels around the country. "There's nothing there except an incredible passion for cricket," he gushed in 2011. "There are children without shoes, without proper equipment, and they're still playing."

Two things in particular stand out about Iranian cricket. The first is that there are almost two entirely separate geographical cricket cultures. The first is centred on Teheran and is almost wholly comprised of expats. Iranian cricket was born in the capital when it arrived with British oil workers in the 1920s. The nationalisation of the Iranian oil industry in 1951 – leading to embargoes and blockades by the suddenly ousted Anglo-Iranian Oil Company and, two years later, a coup instigated by the British and Americans – meant those cricketers left the country (in a bit of a hurry, presumably) and the game effectively died. However, immigrants from Pakistan and India arrived and, from the 1980s onwards, the game was played regularly in the capital. In Teheran today the game is almost exclusively an expat activity.

It's away from the capital, though, that the real magic happens. Most of Iran's indigenous cricketers are from the south-east of the country, and the regions of Chabahar and Baluchistan in particular. Despite the absence of facilities and a shortage of usable equipment, cricket is increasingly popular in the region and the Iranian Cricket Association – who broke from its former parent the baseball federation and successfully attained ICC Affiliate status in 2003 – is making concerted efforts to provide coaching and gear, particularly in schools. In 2013 the ICA also announced an initiative in schools in the Kurdish region in the west of the country. While the Iranian national team is yet to set the world alight, the ICA is a young federation with limited resources ministering to a massive country but, with a growing passion for the game and gifted people like Iqbal Sikander involved in bringing the game into Iranian schools, we should see the benefits filtering up to the national side within a generation or two.

Where Iranian cricket is perhaps most remarkable is in the women's game. As the 2012 *Wisden* reported, there are women's teams active in eight of Iran's 31 provinces, a ratio that is far more impressive when you consider that most of those are the large provinces of the south-east. In Kerman, close to the border with Iraq, there are more women cricketers than men.

Iran is also unique in that it has more qualified women umpires than men. The 2012 Almanack highlighted Narges Lafooti who, in 2010 at the age of just 31, became the first Iranian woman to travel unaccompanied to an overseas sporting event when she officiated at the 2010 Under-19 Women's Championship in Singapore. Lafooti, who also travels the country hosting umpiring courses, is such a highly regarded umpire that often she officiates at the bowler's end for every over. On her first umpire training course in 2003 she was the only woman among 20 men and had no on-field experience at the time, yet still came top of the class with 99%. A gifted sportswoman – she has also captained and coached the Iranian women's rugby team as well as playing cricket and baseball to a high level – she is something of an Iranian sporting pioneer.

Why is cricket so popular among the women of Iran? It's not as simple as a basic love of hitting a ball with a bat, alas; the reasons lie in Iranian culture itself. Cricket is deemed appropriate as it's a game the players can play while still observing the strict dress codes for women. Lafooti is on record as being "tired" of answering questions about the women's dress code, and says the players are happy with what they wear, even going so far as to say the questions are "not polite". She's hardly going to say anything else in the circumstances but, as long as women like Narges Lafooti and her cricket cohorts are making names for themselves against the odds, it wouldn't matter if they took the field in potato sacks.

IRAQ

The Australian "Digger" in desert army fatigues takes strike with his red plastic bat, his rifle and pistol a handy arm's length away (making intimidation of batsmen a risky enterprise). When a dust storm blows up, the "pang" of the tennis ball hitting the empty ration drum which serves as stumps is his only way of knowing his fate, or even if a ball has been bowled, let alone picking what his British or American coalition comrades have bowled. That's if he's not running for cover to make way for an incoming chopper to land on the pitch, the American general's helipad. The threat of inconsistent bounce on the hessian cover is negated by the batsman's love of the big hit, necessary because the ball decelerates very quickly on the dusty outfield. This is especially true of the Americans who make up the numbers if we are short for Australia v England. They are also the subject of accusations of chucking. Normal standards are further watered down at the indoor matches held in the cavernous 30-room North Palace in Baghdad, untouched by looters and occupied by troops of the Royal Australian Navy. Under the gaze of busts of Saddam Hussein in heroic poses, games are played in the ballroom-sized anteroom. A ball landing on the first landing of the massive marble staircase is a four, on the second level a six. Our bowlers take aim at the stumps, a garish reproduction 17th-century French reclining lounger placed end-on, making wicketkeepers redundant. Players are given stern pre-match warnings against hitting the throne in the foyer for reasons of cultural sensitivity. At the time of writing, the Baghdad Ashes are to be inaugurated, comprising a 50-calibre bullet case containing the ashes of a broken leg from an equally tasteless reproduction 15th-century chair, used as the wicket for our first game. When the security situation improves, it is hoped we will play on the old cricket pitch, a remnant from the British days. *Lt. Michael Marley* (Royal Australian Navy)

Latest from Iraq: The Baghdad Ashes were abandoned due to dangerous conditions – not from any hazards of war but simply because temperatures were too high and the surface not up to it. The venue was in the grounds of the Palace of Abu Guyarb, now a helipad, and the largest area we could find guaranteed free from mines or unexploded ordnance. The wicket was made up of some wooden doors from a nearby bombed-out building, which provided interesting bounce. And in the absence of protective gear other than combat helmets, it was decided to play for fun rather than putting national honour at stake. Worst of all there was a total alcohol ban in force. *Colin Manson*, **Wisden 2004**

Regardless of how close it is, the reaction is always the same when an explosion reverberates during our regular Friday games at the newly constituted Baghdad Cricket Ground, a converted playground at the back of an old school that is now the British Embassy. There is initial fear, panic and a dash for the nearest hard cover, the interior of the embassy building itself. The scorebook normally reads "Mortar Stopped Play", although the loudest explosion came from a car bomb at a nearby checkpoint. Conveniently, it just so happens that the corridor where we shelter leads to the appropriately named Mortar Inn, the perfect location for a soothing post-match or post-mortar drink. The only time anyone has ever played on was in a different sport – touch rugby – when our commercial officer ran through to score a try after the rest of us had legged it back inside. A Foreign Office CC colleague had the foresight to bring a beach cricket set to Baghdad. The plastic bat is used against a tennis ball specially adapted by Pakistani construction workers who wrapped it tightly in builders' tape to give it extra weight and reduce the bounce; the playground gives some lift just short of a length, occasionally necessitating body armour. The security situation is such that all play is confined to the BCG – there is no way we could

play outside the International Zone (too much of a target) – even if we could find a pitch. And the ground the Americans use for football and touch rugby has a pipe running across it. The BCG is enclosed by a 12ft fence, itself surrounded by an outer wall topped by razor wire. For obvious reasons, what would normally be a six out of the ground is deemed out, although there was conjecture about interpretation of that rule when one of my beautifully flighted off-breaks was despatched on to the roof of the canteen, and ricocheted back to safety off the satellite dish. Other local rules vary, depending on numbers, but are loosely based on indoor cricket: so batsmen can be caught off the wire fence, batsmen bat for a set number of overs losing runs each time they're out, and everyone bowls. The quirkiest obstacle on the field is a ripped and battered pool table by the cover-point boundary. It is used by off-duty Gurkha guards – even during matches. Spectators' facilities include (in addition to the Mortar Inn) two picnic tables, with a small palm tree for shade. We call the table area the Edward Chaplin Stand after the current Ambassador.
Keith Scott, **Wisden 2005**

A short-notice deployment in Iraq is always a challenge, but every deployment presents cricketing opportunities, and this time was no exception. Having served twice before in Iraq and been lucky enough to be involved in the "Ashes in the Desert", I was delighted to be asked to play in the final match prior to the drawdown of the Australian military contingent. And so it was, on April 25, 2008, the 93rd anniversary of the Anzacs' landing at Gallipoli, that a team representing Australia faced a team representing England in Talill, Dhi Qar Province. The day started with a sunrise drumhead service to commemorate the fallen from the Dardanelles and other conflicts, before the boundary rope was laid out and the scorebox erected. The arrival of the Australian armoured vehicles to provide grandstands, and – with tarpaulins thrown up between them –

shade for the spectators, completed the scene around the dusty oval to one side of the military base. Since everyone was in running distance of their body armour and helmet (in case of indirect fire-attack) this was never going to be a normal game of cricket. The scenery was otherworldly too. If Newlands has Table Mountain and The Oval its gasometer, Talill can boast the nearby Ziggurat of Ur – part of a Sumerian temple complex dating back more than 4,000 years. Its form was clearly visible from the middle, as were the machine guns and 30mm cannons of the grandstands; the roar of helicopters was never far away. The match was hard-fought but ultimately one-sided, as a superb all-round display from the Australians combined with temperatures in excess of 50°C to leave the English wilting. *Andrew Banks*, **Wisden 2009**

ISRAEL

The year began splendidly when Israel received the ICC's coveted "Spirit of Cricket" award in honour of its project involving children from the Bedouin towns of Beersheba, the so-called "Capital of the Negev" (the desert in the south of the country), and Hura. The project is the product of the tireless work done by George Sheader, the youth development officer in the south, and involves using cricket to bring together people from different backgrounds. The senior side performed reasonably well in the European Division Two competition in Guernsey, but not even excellent wins over Gibraltar and Germany could make up for the careless three-run defeat in the first game against Norway after Israel needed 14 with five wickets in hand. Despite that, Eshkol Solomon compiled the competition's highest score, 120 against Gibraltar, and Josh Evans, a promising 17-year-old, took nine wickets in 42 overs of tidy leg-spin. Raanana – boasting six players under 21 – won their first national league title in 20 years under the leadership of former national captain Steven Shein, while the T20 Cup was won by Sri Lanka Jerusalem who, along with Sri Lanka Tel Aviv, were promoted to the A Division. Improvements were made to the fields in Eilat, Diomona and Beersheba, and a modern lecture room with sophisticated camera equipment was installed in the Beersheba clubhouse with the help of the European Cricket Council. Youth cricket is flourishing under the direction of Herschel Gutman, with numbers trebling and women's cricket taking off. Action cricket, played indoors on basketball courts with games lasting 90 minutes, has been introduced on Thursday and Saturday nights: 13 teams take part and the competition has been hailed in the local press. On December 12, a group of 35 Palestinian scholars, aged between eight and 12, from the West Bank villages of Samoa and Yaata travelled to Beersheba to meet fellow students from Yerucham and Dimona. For four hours, the boys and girls – who had never met before – played cricket together, and will continue to meet once a month in a project put together by the Israel Cricket Association. Al Quds and the Peres Centre for Peace. The project is being financed by an anonymous donor from England. *Stanley Perlman*, **Wisden 2011**

"When holding a cricket bat, I feel I hold the whole world."

Sixteen-year-old Shehadeh Salamin was one of the Palestinians involved in the initiative to bring Israeli and Palestinian children together through the enjoyment of cricket. As quotes go, it's a cracker on several levels: expressing in a dozen words not only what the scheme is about but also the potential cricket has for uniting the divided and acting as a vehicle for hopes and dreams.

Cricket4Peace is a fantastic initiative. Launched only in 2010, the idea is that around 80 boys and girls, Palestinian and Jewish, from four different places are brought together to play cricket. Shehadeh, shouting his global cricketing message from the village of al-Samoa, where he lives in the West Bank, was one of those kids. He'd always dreamed of being a famous Palestinian footballer, but once cricket arrived in al-Samoa there was only one sport for him. "The game rapidly became our flagship sport, with most kids preferring cricket over football," he said. But, for all their enthusiasm, Shehadeh and his friends found it hard to get better at the game when they were just playing among themselves. They needed to spread their wings to improve.

When Cricket4Peace suggested they get together with some Israeli kids to play, Shehadeh was worried. "I must admit, I had concerns," he said. "However, when we reached Beersheba, the Israeli coach, George, greeted us with kindness and his warm words broke the barrier of fear in me. I thought to myself, I like to play cricket just like Israeli children. It would be fun to play together."

Sharon Gudker hails from the other side of the divide. She was there when the bus from al-Samoa turned up and its passengers disembarked and, like Shehadeh, she was apprehensive.

"I watched them getting off the bus and they all looked so different to us," she recalled. "I was very nervous; even a bit scared to shake their hands."

There was also an English team there for the combined Israeli and Palestinian kids to play against. "I wasn't picked to play against the English, but it was a very strange feeling cheering the Palestinian kids each time they scored a run or took a wicket," said Sharon. "It was as if it didn't matter that they were Palestinians because we were all playing together on the same team."

The combined team won by one run and the celebrations were predictably euphoric.

A similar project teaches cricket to Bedouin children, overseen by Israel Cricket Association president and long-serving *Wisden* contributor Stanley Perlman, and run by the British charity Cricket for Change. They've taught hundreds of children from Beersheba alone, and have brought in Bedouin children from the Negev desert to teach the game to them as well as encouraging them all to mingle – scenes that would have been beyond the wildest dreams of the most idealistic cricket fan a few years ago, let alone back in the days when cricket was introduced to Israel.

Cricket was a fairly popular sport before 1948, with regular matches in Jerusalem, Haifa and the Tel-Hashoma army camp but, when the British left after the creation of the Israeli state, the game went into a decline. It didn't vanish altogether, however, and the first recorded all-Israeli match took place in 1954 when a team from Tel Aviv took on a Beersheba side that contained a father and his seven sons. At least the scorers could have a decent stab at the bowler's name whenever a new man marked out his run.

The game was struggling to survive in the early- and mid-1960s, but by the end of the decade the influx of Jewish immigrants from cricket-playing countries meant the sport was hauled back from the brink. A league began in 1966, and the Israeli Cricket Association was founded two years later. There was a further boost to cricket in the country when visiting teams began showing up with some pretty illustrious players. Ken Barrington arrived in 1968 with Bournemouth CC, who became the first overseas team to tour Israel. The tour took place not long after the Six Day War but, despite wading into a very recent trauma, Barrington made a hundred and was such a hit with the locals that he was elected the first president of the Israeli Cricket Supporters' Association. Three years later Harrow CC turned up with Basil D'Oliveira in tow.

The national team made steady progress, albeit sometimes in the face of political protests. They competed in their first ICC Trophy tournament just before the World Cup in Birmingham in 1979 (the same year in which Sri Lanka refused to play them for political reasons), but it took until 1990 for Israel to register its first win in that competition (from which the leading sides progress to the World Cup proper), a one-wicket thriller against Argentina in the Netherlands.

In 1997, buoyed by progress in the Middle East peace talks, Malaysia allowed Israel to compete in the ICC Trophy in Kuala Lumpur. This was quite something, as Malaysia had never recognised Israel as a sovereign state and had even banned its citizens from fraternising with Israelis. Despite the more relaxed regulations and atmosphere, when Israel played Gibraltar in their first match a group of around 500 demonstrators charged into the ground, on to the pitch and set about smashing advertising hoardings and lighting bonfires on the outfield. The only thing was, having suspected that something like this was in the offing, the authorities had switched the Israel game to another venue, leaving the protestors confronted by nothing more than the bewildered-looking cricketers of Canada and the Netherlands. Meanwhile, across town, Israel and Gibraltar played out their game in front of a handful of spectators and a hundred bored riot police lounging in the sunshine.

The nature of the game of cricket means that the leap from rioting Malaysians to joyful Israeli and Palestinian children celebrating a thrilling win on the cricket field isn't such a large one. Discord and protest will follow Israel wherever it goes but, as long as there are initiatives like those recognised above by the ICC, then cricket will continue to have a positive influence. It might not change the world – or even solve the Middle East conflict – but as long as kids like Shehadeh can feel like they have the world in their hands when wielding 2lb 8oz of English willow, then there's surely optimism for the future.

ITALY

In contrast with 1992, 1993 was the happiest year in the brief history of Italian cricket and fittingly marked the bicentenary of the first recorded game in the peninsula. The celebrations included a tour by MCC, who won all their games except the two-day match against the national side, when they struggled to earn a draw. Cesena retained the championship and also triumphed in the European Club Championship on their home ground, the Ippodromo del Sevio. Having beaten the Greek champions Phaeax and the Austrian champions Vienna, the home team then beat the holders, Château de Thoiry, by eight wickets thanks to a century by Sunandra Pearis. Italy's ambition in 1994 is to become the first ICC Affiliate to be upgraded to Associate Membership. *Simone Gambino*, **Wisden 1994**

Having lent his name to a well-known piece of cricketing slang – not to mention his wide and varied travels – it's fitting that Horatio Nelson should appear in these pages, albeit through an allusion rather than a direct citation. Arguably the most appropriate game of the tour to mark the bicentenary of Italian cricket took place a week earlier, when the tourists beat the United Nations Cricket Club at Carney Park in Naples, for it was in Naples that the first recorded cricket was played in Italy, when men from the crew of Nelson's frigate HMS *Agamemnon* went ashore with bat and ball. Some sources claim that Nelson himself organised the game; certainly he would have at least granted the shore leave for it even if he wasn't actually picking the sides and collecting the match fees. Captain Nelson, as he was then, would have been in good spirits at the time, and possibly well-disposed towards the idea of his crew indulging in a bit of healthy sporting endeavour: the *Agamemnon* was his first command in five frustrating land-lubbing years, and during the few days he was moored at Naples he met Emma Hamilton for the first time, the wife of the British ambassador to the Court of Naples who would famously become his mistress.

We don't know for certain if Nelson was a cricket fan – a plaque at Mitcham Cricket Club suggests that he watched the game there while living nearby at Merton in a bizarre *ménage à trois* with the Hamiltons – but at this stage in his life he still had the eye, the arm and presumably the third part of his anatomy that makes the score 111 a 'Nelson'.

Cricket in Italy has been booming in recent years thanks to the arrival of immigrants from the Test nations, particularly India, Pakistan, Sri Lanka and Bangladesh. The Italian national league boasts 33 teams divided into three divisions, and on summer afternoons green spaces in towns and cities across the nation are filled with young Asian men playing games of cricket. The Italian national side, which more than holds its own among the leading European teams, has always featured a number of players of Asian origin; players like Sri Lankan-born Gayashan Munasinghe, who first played for the Italian team at the age of 21 in 2008 not long after arriving in Rome from Colombo with his father, a policeman in Sri Lanka but a pastry chef in the Eternal City.

"I struggled to fit in when I arrived," he said in 2008, "but I am now proud to represent Italy."

High-profile Italian politicians – including Silvio Berlusconi when he was prime minister – have spoken out against immigration despite Italy's declining population, but the proliferation of impromptu yet highly sophisticated matches involving young Asian men across Italy suggests that the cricket-playing migrant is there to stay. Not only that, he can play a pretty decent off-drive too.

If Berlusconi ever saw one of these keenly contested pick-up games when being ferried between courthouse, parliament and bunga bunga party, and if he had any inkling what they were, he might have reflected how AC Milan – the football club he owns that has won the European Cup and Champions League seven times – actually started out in 1899 as the Milan Football and Cricket Club, formed by a small group of British expat industrialists looking to recreate a sporting taste of home. Six years earlier the Genoa Cricket and Athletic Club had become Italy's first cricket club, and today they too are another successful football club.

Neither has had a cricket section for many years. The game in Italy had been declining steadily since the Second World War when, in the 1960s, diplomats and embassy staff from traditional cricket nations began to revive it. While it would have been easy to just play among themselves, these modern pioneers made sure there was a quota of Italians in each team for each game. The fruits of this policy can be seen today, with most club teams having mainly Italian names on their teamsheets. In the 2006 *Wisden* Simone Gambino noted that when Pianoro won the Italian Cup the previous season there were eight Italians in their side.

A number of cricketers fought in Italy during the Second World War, including Hedley Verity, arguably the greatest spin bowler England ever produced, who was seriously wounded in Sicily and who died and is buried at Caserta. Ted Dexter was born and raised in Milan, where his father was a successful insurance broker. When he travelled between home and boarding school in England Dexter would make the journey on the Orient Express.

Another cricket legend with Italian connections is Donald Bradman. It was discovered recently that The Don had an Italian great-grandfather, and a pretty colourful one at that. Emmanuel Danero was born in Genoa in 1807, 86 years before Italy's first cricket club would be founded there. A sailor by profession, Danero emigrated to Australia in 1826 to run hotels in Sydney. Married three times, Danero fathered an astonishing 25 children, one of whom, an illegitimate daughter, was Bradman's grandmother.

Bradman's Italian connection doesn't end there either: when the British Army needed a code phrase to signal the start of the assault on Monte Cassino, they used, "Bradman will be batting tomorrow." It wasn't "England expects ..." by any means, but the man who had apparently introduced cricket to Italy would probably have approved.

JAPAN

Though expatriates still account for the bulk of cricket played in Japan, the game is now being played all over the country and locals are gaining in numbers and enthusiasm. We are seeing at least one new university team a year, and all but two of the positions in the Japan Cricket Association are now held by Japanese. Japan's only cricket magazine, *The Straight Bat*, sponsored a competition of two-day matches, with five teams entered. The winning team, Tokyo Bay CC, was founded only two years ago by one of the new pioneers of Japanese cricket, Fumito Miyakawa. Having previously experienced only 35-over cricket, it took some time for the locals to become accustomed to the longer game, but Mr Miyakawa, who had been to New Zealand to study cricket, led his team to a well-deserved victory over Senshu University. *The Straight Bat* also sponsored the second annual Challenge Cup for beginners, with 65 players vying for honours. The cup was won by Ms Miki Koyama for her dedication, enthusiasm and all-round cricket skills. The Yokohama Country and Athletic Club's fourth annual six-a-side competition had to be held over two days to accommodate all those who wanted to play, and even then some missed out; victory went for the second year running to the Edogawa Falcons. The season ended with a bang when Jeff Thomson came to Tokyo and conducted three days of coaching on behalf of the JCA. *Trevor Bayley*, **Wisden 1995**

KAZAKHSTAN

Western expats have come and gone over the 16 years since the former Soviet Republic of Kazakhstan became independent. But, with the capital Almaty now established as the boom town of Central Asia, there is a settled Indian and Pakistani community, and about 15 regular players. This is a place of extreme temperature, ranging from 40°C in summer to −40°C in winter. But summer days can be favourable for cricket, and the game began regularly in 1995 with makeshift equipment made from boxes and broom handles. Now the ACC (Almaty Cricket Club) has real wickets, a couple of brand-new bats, a supply of tape-balls and official permission to play at weekends on the tarmac playground at School No. 130. It is inevitably a little makeshift: no runs behind the wicket (the school is there), bowling only to one end, two runs awarded if the ball goes into the bushes inside the boundary; and no lbws − too many arguments. But there is a strong community spirit behind the whole project, with benefits to the school: the grass is being mown, and six wooden benches have been placed nearby where old people can sit. Mostly, however, the locals just peer out, bemused, from the Soviet-era apartment blocks overlooking the ground. *Roger Holland*, **Wisden 2007**

KIRIBATI

Cricket in the Republic of Kiribati – 33 fragmented and isolated South Pacific atolls that used to be called the Gilbert Islands – dates back to the arrival of the British in 1892. The game has now dwindled to two or three matches a year, between an Australian XI and the Rest of the World, on a ground of white coral sand with no shade from the burning sun, other than the odd passing frigate bird. The eccentricities of early cricket here were recorded in Arthur Grimble's *A Pattern of Islands*. The most dramatic event of recent years came when the Kiribati XI flew to play an away fixture against the Republic of Tuvalu, formerly the Ellice Islands. Batting second, Kiribati were down to the last pair and needed six to win off the last ball. Darkness was falling fast and pressure mounting in more ways than one – the plane for the return journey had to take off from a narrow strip of land, between the sea and the lagoon, with no landing lights. The batsman on strike was a strapping player called Tapatulu, a man of fearsome strength renowned locally for having once been lost at sea in a canoe for three months. It was a good-length ball. Tapatulu took a step outside leg stump and, with the well-used "Len Hutton" team bat, despatched the ball over cow corner for six. *David de Silva*, **Wisden 1997**

The name Kiribati is derived from the local pronunciation of the islands' former name of the Gilbert Islands, in turn taken from Captain Thomas Gilbert of the *Charlotte* who, on returning from the first-ever voyage transporting convicts from Britain to Australia, sailed through them on the way home in 1788. The first British settlers arrived in 1837, and the islands formally became a British protectorate along with the nearby Ellice Islands in 1892.

Thirteen years later Arthur Grimble arrived as a cadet administrative officer working for the British Foreign Office and stayed for six years, recording his experiences in his terrific memoir *A Pattern of Islands*, published in 1952. In it he details the early history of cricket on the

Gilberts in a humorous prose so dry the pages almost become brittle in your hands. Grimble was a decent cricketer himself – he captained both the Chigwell School and Magdalene College teams – and his knowledge of and love for both the game and the islands shines through his prose.

"The beginnings of cricket in the Pacific were not invariably attended by the spirit of brotherhood that this noble sport was once believed to inspire," he wrote. "A match there was an affair of hundreds, not elevens; no tally of sides was kept, no amiable warnings of visits were issued; one village simply arose on a day and set forth to give battle to another. 'Battle' is the key word. The marching crowd paraded around the village of its chosen enemies with taunts and brandished bats until these emerged to accept the challenge … Those earliest Samoan matches lasted for weeks at a time and often ended in considerable slaughter. It was excellent for courage but poor for the moral scoreboard."

Similar scenes can be found to this day, I believe, in some of the more competitive Yorkshire leagues.

From this passage alone it's easy to see where Tapatulu's power hitting and cool-as-a-cucumber big-match temperament derived, as exhibited in the match with Tuvalu mentioned above. When you come from a cricketing culture of cracked skulls and mass brawls, hitting a six from the last ball while your transport home revs its engines isn't half as much of a challenge as it might sound.

Like most of the Cricket Round the World correspondents of today, Grimble described some of the more idiosyncratic local challenges he faced while engaged in promoting cricket on the islands and described them brilliantly. The grass on the outfield, for example, was far from ideal, being dry, coarse and clumped in tussocks and tufts, inevitably influencing the style of cricket.

"The consequence was we all became deliberate moon-shooters and cow-shooters," he recalled. "It was deeply immoral cricket and, for that very reason, highly amusing. Nevertheless, I preferred the stone age, when a batsman could score along the ground and even a wicked fluke off the edge of the bat could roll as sweetly (for me) to the boundary as the most accomplished leg-glance."

Coaching also threw up challenges. After one session he noticed one of the locals was a little tight-lipped when he canvassed him about scheduling the next practice.

"I explained that there was no enforcement, but put it to him that the game was a good game: didn't he think so too? 'Sir,' he said again, 'we do not wish to deceive you. It seems to us a very exhausting game. It makes our hearts die inside us.'"

Again there's a global resonance here, for who among us hasn't had a similar reaction from a partner on asking whether he or she fancies coming to watch us play for the sixth summer weekend in succession?

My favourite part of Grimble's book is also one of my favourite passages of writing of any kind on the subject of cricket, even if he is talking about the Pacific *kirikiti* version of the game. It also sums up the appeal and success of the Cricket Round the World section itself: those universal aspects of the game – the ubiquitous truths that lie way beyond the laws and the scorebook – that are the key to the game taking hold even in the most unlikely of surroundings.

"But I like best of all the dictum of an old man of the Sun clan," wrote Grimble, "who once said to me, 'We old men take joy in watching the *kirikiti* of our grandsons, because it is a fighting between factions which makes the fighters love each other' ... I doubt if anyone of more sophisticated culture has ever summed up the spiritual value of cricket in more telling words than his. 'Spiritual' may sound over-sentimental to a modern generation, but I stand by it, as everyone else will who has witnessed the moral teaching-force of the game in malarial jungle, or sandy desolation, or the uttermost islands of the sea."

KOSOVO

It may be surprising to learn that cricket was played in Kosovo, a country which declared its independence as recently as February 2008, by previous generations – or at least something resembling cricket. The pastime of *guxha* (pronounced "goojah") was a traditional game now largely replaced among young Kosovars' affections by football. But Dritan, a Kosovar living in Brighton, realised there was something familiar about the game being played down the road from his home at the County Ground in Hove. "I remember my father playing *guxha*, and I have since seen cricket being played here, and there are similarities between the skills and the way of scoring," he said. Inevitably, the more conventional version of the game arrived with the influx of armed forces during the conflict in Kosovo in the late 1990s, and expats of virtually every Test nation played in the UNMIK (United Nations Mission In Kosovo) gym in Pristina using a taped-up tennis ball and a home-made bat. Encouraged perhaps by the presence of Major-General Garry Robison, who was on peacekeeping duties in the country and is the current chairman of combined services cricket, the ICC also ventured into Kosovo, staging a "Spirit of Cricket" weekend in February 2002 at the national stadium in Pristina – which was said to have been used to detain 10,000 Albanians during the height of the conflict. As well as introducing the game to Serbian and Albanian children as a means of breaking down barriers between the communities, there was a 15-over match between The Princess of Wales's Royal Regiment, the forces champions at the time, and the Indian personnel of UNMIK. More recently, a team of Gurkhas based in Pristina travelled to Skopje to take part in a three-team Twenty20 tournament along with a KFOR (Kosovo Force) side in June 2007. The Gurkhas began by putting on an excellent display of military prowess with the "presentation of the *kukri*", although they lost one of their star players, who managed to slash his own arm with a *kukri* (knife) during the pre-match ritual. It mattered little, as the Gurkhas claimed victory thanks to the performance of Rifleman Chandrakumar Limbu-by-Prasad Chamarty, whose name troubled the scorers almost as much as his runs did. *Timothy Abraham,* **Wisden 2010**

LESOTHO

The old heavy roller lies alone and desolate on the edge of what used to be Lesotho's main cricket ground, alongside the Maseru Club. It is all that remains of the game that once thrived among British expatriates in the old protectorate of Basutoland, totally surrounded by South Africa. Other cricketing bits and pieces were carted over the South African border, and the field is now devoted to football, with the roller looking on forlornly. But cricket is clinging on: it is played on Sunday afternoons on roll-out matting on a local college field. The most regular players now are Asian expatriates, but the game has picked up among youngsters of school age, both boys and girls. Lesotho ranks officially among the ICC's Affiliate countries, along with the likes of Ghana, Malawi and Mozambique; but when Mozambique paid a visit to Lesotho in mid-2005, they were far superior to a team with ten Basotho players. Despite this, Lesotho Cricket Association chairman Majorobela Sakoane is full of optimism: "We hit bottom and now we're beginning to climb again," he says. *Colin Macbeth*, **Wisden 2006**

LUXEMBOURG

An exceptionally warm and dry summer in the Grand Duchy saw the inauguration of a national league. Over 80 players took part in ten matches, as the Optimists pipped the Communities to the title. Black Stuff, Euratom and the Maidens completed the line-up and new teams have applied to join in 2000. Just as importantly, the first-ever conversation at the wicket in Letztebuergesch – a dialect that has much in common with Flemish and German – took place between two Black Stuff batsmen, even though the club is theoretically drawn from the Irish community. The Optimists also took part in the Belgian League, and came fifth in the first division ensuring they will stay there when the format changes next season. The loss of the prolific William Heath was made up for by Aamer bin Jung, who averaged nearly 90, but the bowlers were often let down by some poor catching. It was also a big year for Optimists president Pierre Wener, the "father of the euro", whose brainchild was finally born. MCC last visited Luxembourg in 1992, and are coming again in August 2000. Since the visit eight years ago, the Stade Prince Henri and the Pavillon Cricket have been built, and the future of Luxembourg cricket has grown more secure. This year, however, three international matches were disappointingly lost: one to France, and two to Switzerland. Cricket formally appeared at the European School for the first time, and evening cricket continued to attract keen interest. Among teams to play this year were the social (Britannia Pub, Hash Harriers, the George and Dragon), the financial (Flemings, the Court of Auditors), and the apparently extra-terrestrial (Astra Satellites). Court of Auditors boasted eight nationalities on one occasion, a genuine reflection of this cosmopolitan society. But the best witness to this was the claim of a Danish translator at the European Parliament to be the grandson of Ellis Achong, the Trinidadian originator of the Chinaman. *Adrian Wykes*, **Wisden 2000**

MALI

Cricket has now nudged closer to what might be its ultimate destination: Timbuktu. From unlikely beginnings in one school's English Club in 2001 (following a chance remark by the British consul Violet Diallo), cricket has been introduced into ten schools across Bamako, the capital of Mali. Unfortunately few people have a clue where Mali is. ("You mean Bali?" "No, it's in Africa." "Ah, Malawi!" "No! M–A–L–I. It's in *West* Africa!") It's a poor, sand-rich, land-locked country with an extraordinarily rich cultural heritage. But since it's a former French colony, that heritage does not include cricket. Or it didn't. Malians established their cricket association, AMaCrik, in 2003, and the first inter-school tournament took place in 2004. When shown models of bats and asked to produce something similar, a local carpenter said, "Yes of course … but what are they?" The carpenter, Yacouba Coulibaly, has since scaled a steep learning curve, producing wooden bats and wickets for us; and thanks to some generous donations we now have some sets of "real" kit. But they are hard to get and expensive to transport here. The climate is unyielding, and we play a lot on sand and rock. Even so, regular turnout at Saturday-morning training sessions in Bamako now exceeds 90 people, and there are early developments in other towns. "When you hear it explained, you may not see why people like cricket," said one teacher, "but once you start playing then you get hooked." This teacher is now AMaCrik's president. Timbuktu? (Officially it's Tombouctou.) It's more than 900km from Bamako, but we are heading in that direction. *Phil Watson*, **Wisden 2005**

MEXICO

What is said to be the oldest surviving sports photograph in Mexico, dating from 1865, shows a cricket team with Emperor Maximilian in their midst, and Mexico City CC, founded in 1894, has been playing on its present site for 40 years. The ground at the Reforma Club is picturesque – with a lush outfield set among giant eucalyptus trees – and the club is particularly vibrant and sociable. At 7,200ft above sea level, it is believed to be the second-highest turf wicket in the world. At present more than 150 cricketers play in competitions every year, between October and March. There is also now an Australian coach, Elliot Cartledge. In 2000 the club hosted touring teams from Belize, Memorial CC of Houston (for the 15th successive year) and the British and Dominion Club of Los Angeles. Although the game was introduced to Mexico by the English, the club has outgrown these roots and embraces players from all backgrounds and abilities. *Keith Foster*, **Wisden 2001**

There is a tangible sadness about the 1865 photograph of Maximilian I standing among cricketers. Like much of the 19th century, the period around 1865 was a turbulent one in Mexican history and it had been hoped that the installation of the Habsburg prince – with the backing of Napoleon III and Mexican monarchists – might bring stability to the region. When the photograph was taken Maximilian had been in Mexico for less than a year, and was trying hard to make a difference despite the constant battles between his French troops and Benito Juarez's liberal forces. Shocked by the poverty and hardship he saw in Mexico City, Maximilian cut working hours, abolished child labour and cancelled any debts over ten pesos owed by Mexican workers. Despite all this he found himself opposed and frustrated at every turn, and the neighbouring United States refused even to recognise his rule.

The cricket match must have provided a rare moment of relief and relaxation for him. The photograph, now in the Musée Royal de l'Armée in Brussels, shows a peaceful scene, 22 players spread out in a line along the pitch during a break in play. Maximilian himself is standing by the stumps in shirt-sleeves and white trousers, suggesting that he was most likely playing in the game himself. There couldn't have been a greater contrast between the cut-and-thrust of 19th-century Mexican politics, the social problems he was trying to tackle head on, not to mention very real danger of overthrow and assassination, and the chance to spend an afternoon on the cricket field where nothing mattered but the score and the exhilaration of playing the game.

In the months that followed the photograph being taken, Napoleon III would withdraw his troops for more pressing matters in Europe, leaving Maximilian exposed and facing inevitable downfall. His wife Carlotta travelled to Europe, flitting from palace to palace, begging in vain for assistance. But, having refused to leave Mexico himself and fighting a determined but futile rearguard action with depleted forces, Maximilian was eventually captured by Juarez's troops and executed by firing squad in May 1867 at the age of just 34.

The 1865 photograph is a typical one of the age, all self-conscious chest-puffing, rigid poses and austere faces granite-still behind elaborate facial hair. A couple of players lounge on the ground, most are standing. Maximilian is at the centre, surrounded for once by people he could trust and with whom he could relax. Whether it was the only game he played or was one of many, the calmness of the scene and the knowledge that he had less than two years to live lends it extra poignancy, a rare moment of peace in three turbulent and ultimately tragic years.

It's likely that the location of shot is the ground at Napoles. We have a terrific description of cricket there around that time from William Henry Bullock in his 1865 book *Around Mexico*. If the earliest *Wisdens* had contained a Cricket Round the World section instead of the rules of quoits and lists of canals, there's every chance this would have been in there: in style and content it wouldn't even be greatly out of place in the Almanack today.

"During the voyage out from England I had heard that cricket was played in the country, but supposed it would turn out to be cricket of that degenerate sort which one finds occasionally played by the English residents in different parts of Europe," Bullock wrote. "So that when I got to the ground, and found an excellent pavilion, a scoring box, visitors' tent, the field marked out with flags with the well-known letters MCC (Mexico, not Marylebone, Cricket Club) marked upon them, and some 18 or 20 players in flannels and cricket shoes, I was a little astonished, and soon found out that I had to do with a very different sort of cricket to what I had expected. Perhaps the most surprising part of the performance was that the best player on the ground was a Mexican, whose bowling and batting did infinite credit to the training which he received at Brice Castle School.

"Among the English players were several gentlemen close upon 60 years of age, who all expressed to me their conviction that they owe much of the health and energy which they still possessed, in spite of 40 years' residence in Mexico, to having stuck through thick and thin to their Sunday cricket. They assured me that they had never allowed political events to interfere with their game which they had pursued unconcernedly, more than once, in view of the fighting going on in the hills around them.

"Being fully alive to the fact that cricket is nothing without beer, there is always a liberal supply on the ground, of a very excellent quality, supplied by the firm of Blackmore – a name revered, beyond all others, by Englishmen in Mexico."

At the time of Bullock's visit, as hinted at by the players he spoke to, cricket was already well established in Mexico. In fact there is documented evidence that the game was being played there as far back as 1827. Found recently among the papers of Daniel and Lewis Price, brother traders in Mexico in the 1820s, was an 1838 pamphlet produced by the Mexico Union Cricket Club. It contains a wealth of information about the club, including the anniversary dinner held on February 21, 1838, to mark the 11th birthday of the club, confirming Mexico Union as one of the earliest cricket clubs in the world, and certainly one of the oldest outside Britain.

The Union took its cricket seriously too: dress code was strictly flannel jacket, white trousers and a straw hat, and anyone found on or near the pitch on match-day in unsuitable attire was liable to a fine of two dollars. There were also fines for lateness (matches commenced at 8am), failing to turn up for matches and even for withdrawing from games without written notice at least two days in advance.

The list of members' names betrays the expat nature of the club; most of the members are diplomats and merchants. One perhaps surprising inclusion is that of Joel Roberts Poinsett, who was appointed the United States' first-ever Minister to Mexico in 1825. Poinsett was known at the time for his fiercely anti-British standpoint, so to find him listed as a member of a club devoted to the most British of games is a curious thing. Maybe he set politics aside at the weekends; maybe he was just in a good mood and well disposed towards humanity in general, having just discovered south of Mexico City the plant known to this day as the poinsettia.

MONGOLIA

It started with a Scotsman, Wilf McKee, who gradually collected the kit and the trophy. In 2002 and 2003, there were season-long competitions between India and the Rest of the World, with over 20 regulars. Every week, the match was written up in the *Ulaanbaatar Post*, the local English-language newspaper. The September finals, played in the National Stadium, used the same bit of grass where enormous Mongolian wrestlers had just been fighting for the national championship: nice stadium, uneven bounce. Everyone played with the abandon of beginners; running between the wickets was joyous and selfish, as the *UB Post* reported. "We were entertained with one of the typical and traditional spectacular run-outs that combine lunacy, beauty and tragedy in a few anarchic seconds, bringing tears to the eyes of even the most hardened observers." Cricket continues now, but less regularly. And we have never equalled Mongolia's only golf course in terms of harnessing the locals' skills. Due to the length of the course they employed mounted spotters, who charged away on horseback after every drive to follow the ball's path. Our outfield, after the rain starts, is so slow that the only way of getting the ball anywhere is heaving it up in the air and aiming for a fielder who can't catch. The weather is unpredictable, and dust storms, snow and violent thunder can all appear rapidly from a clear sky, but the surrounding mountains make for a spectacular backdrop whatever the weather. Other local factors: anybody who bowls fast to a newcomer is looked down upon; underarm bowling is allowed; it is difficult to make the Americans not throw the bat away after hitting and to run straight instead of in circles (one Mongolian hit the ball and ran to the fence to get his four runs); catches are dropped deliberately to make the game interesting and chivalrous. We do allow beers and smokes on the field. *Richard Sandali and Babu Joseph*, **Wisden 2006**

If Mongolia has anything going for it in cricket terms, it's space. With a population density of just five people per square mile – the lowest in the world – in a nation of more than 600,000 square miles, you shouldn't in theory take too long to find somewhere to bash a set of stumps into the ground and start picking sides. However, the game has struggled to take any kind of hold since the entry above, and that's despite the enthusiasm that bursts out of every sentence.

Where some countries seem to take naturally to cricket despite there being no history there, others don't. Not in the slightest. Some people can be won over by others' clear love for the game or just satisfy a curiosity piqued by watching the foreigners going about their weird sport in the park.

None of this appears to have happened in Mongolia. Admittedly the prevailing meteorology makes cricket viable only three months a year, but there's more to it than that. It could be because there's no tradition of stick sports out there in the middle of Asia. The Mongolians love their wrestling, their archery and their horse racing above all else. Mongol history and culture are steeped in all three and have been since the days of Genghis Khan. Not for nothing do those three events make up the Naadam festival each year in Ulaanbaatar, which is also known as *ereen gurvan naadam*, or the "three games of men". In July each year the Naadam stadium, where the cricketers above were fortunate to be allowed to play, is filled to capacity to watch a festival of manliness.

Maybe cricket – with its long pauses, gentle rhythms and limited opportunities to have a good roar and shout – just doesn't suit the Mongolian temperament. In addition Wilf McKee seems to have disappeared from the cricket scene, although the Mongolian Cricket Club is still going, and there was talk a couple of years ago of an Ulaanbaatar cricket club too, but it seems at the moment that if the game survives at all it's purely an expat activity.

MYANMAR

Viewed by many as a throwback to the country's colonial past, cricket here has often struggled for acceptance, and until recently had all but died out. Due to the country's political isolation, it may be some time yet before there is any repeat of the MCC matches against Rangoon Gymkhana and All-Burma in 1926-27 (Maurice Tate had match figures of ten for 72). But, led by one of Myanmar's most famous action movie stars, 65-year-old Nyunt Win, who began playing when he was nine, the game is enjoying a small revival. Through the efforts of some expat Australians, the country's first permanent (and playable) turf wicket was developed in 2003, at the Pun Hlaing Golf Estate in northern Yangon (formerly Rangoon). Due to the weather (it's either pouring with rain or unbearably hot) the season is short, from December to February. But there is a national league, with eight teams containing an eclectic mix of ages and nationalities, playing a 30-over league and knockout and, if time permits before the hot season, a 13-over tournament. We have introduced the game to schools in Yangon and Mandalay, and the children are enthusiastic. The only real international games at present are between the Ayeyarwaddy Cricket Club, based at Pun Hlaing, and the Siam Cricket Club in Bangkok, with the boys from Bangkok winning the Andaman Trophy on their last trip to Yangon. *Stu Bennett,* **Wisden 2006**

NAURU

Half Nauru's active cricketers are Nauruans, a fact that disguises the state of the game on this 21 sq km Pacific island (population 12,000) formed from guano, and once made wealthy by phosphates. Two Sri Lankans, an Australian and three locals carry the flag with irregular net sessions in the world's smallest republic. Australian, Indian and Nauruan elevens used to play regularly on a coir matting wicket with a sandy outfield outside the hospital. The Nauruans displayed high skill levels learnt through exposure to cricket in Victoria, where they worked in the phosphate company's headquarters. However, when phosphate revenues declined, the government slashed the expatriate-laden civil service, hence the recent collapse. But the Sri Lankan organiser, Mervyn Weerasinghe, is confident player numbers can increase as long as he can hold on to the gear: recently one of the coir mats was stolen; the other is now in hiding. *Tony Munro,* **Wisden 2004**

It's not often that politics impinges on Cricket Round the World. Most of the tales are of hard-working associations running leagues, national teams making steady progress, expats baffling locals with their ground fielding and strokeplay, or quirky tours by quirky teams to quirky places. Politics rarely raises its head – in the world of cricket, it's all about the game. Politics is for, well, politicians.

Sometimes, however, cricket and politics come together. They did – and continue to do so – in Nauru, the world's smallest independent republic, a bizarre eight square miles of coral atoll in the Pacific Ocean. This 2004 entry doesn't touch upon it, but in Nauru politics and cricket are absolutely inseparable.

Nauru is a place like no other on earth. Its population of roughly 10,000 lives almost entirely around the coast, as the rest of the island is now a lunar-style wasteland, a forest of lumpy, grey limestone stumps that are the legacy of Nauru's all-but-extinguished phosphate industry. Nauru made a fortune from the millennium's worth of bird droppings that covered the island, but unfortunately it started running out in the 1990s and was all but exhausted by 2006. Nauru depended almost exclusively on phosphate income and, despite winning an eight-figure payout in 1989 when the nation sued Australia, New Zealand and the UK for the environmental damage caused by those nations' companies' mining activities, the place is on its uppers and unemployment is touching 90%. In one of international economics' more bizarre episodes, Nauru even managed to lose £2 million in the 1990s by investing in a London musical about Leonardo da Vinci that closed after five weeks.

Nauru's bleak landscape – 90% of it is or was taken up with phosphate mining – also means fresh food is hard to come by. Nearly everything has to be imported and inevitably that means a diet of processed food high in fat and sugar. Primarily as a result of this Nauru is home to the most obese population in the world: 71% of Nauruans are clinically obese, and an astounding 94.5% of men are classed as overweight, while the island also has the world's highest rates of diabetes. Some researchers believe this is the legacy of Nauru's boom time: they got rich and they got fat, and culturally obesity is seen as a sign of prosperity.

After the turn of the millennium Nauru, broke to the point where the national airline's only aircraft had been repossessed, was presented with a gift horse whose dental work the Nauruan balance sheet forbade close examination. In 2001 a Norwegian freighter, the *Tampa*, was refused permission to enter Australian waters with more than 400 mainly Afghan asylum seekers it had rescued from flimsy boats drifting in the Indian Ocean. After some seat-of-the-pants international diplomacy – and some admirable sticking-to-his-guns by the compassionate Norwegian captain – the refugees were offloaded on to an Australian navy ship and taken to Nauru, where they would be housed in a temporary detention centre while their claims were processed. This led to what became known as Australia's "Pacific Solution", where Nauru – along with Christmas Island and Manus Island, Papua New Guinea – were given millions of dollars in aid in return for hosting the asylum seekers. This bizarre situation ran for six years until 2007.

Originally the refugees were due to be housed in accommodation blocks constructed for an international weightlifting tournament, but that fell through. Instead the bewildered itinerants were housed in old-fashioned heavy canvas soldiers' tents at Topside, on the site of what had been Nauru's national stadium.

All this earned Nauru one hundred million Australian dollars.

Despite being closed by Prime Minister Kevin Rudd when he was elected in 2007, in late 2012 Nauru's detention centre opened again after he'd been removed from office. Today the refugees are mostly Sri Lankans, who have taken to boats in order to reach Australia and a new life. It's an incredibly dangerous crossing, and one can only wonder at the desperation that would prompt anyone to try it, especially when their destination has made it clear they're neither welcome nor wanted. Not only that, the journey is made in the full knowledge that if your leaky, overcrowded boat survives the crossing you'll most likely be picked up in the waters off the Australian coast and transported to the barren landscape of Nauru, where you'll stay until someone in an office somewhere hundreds of miles away finally gets around to considering your application. You could be there for years.

In order to deter potential migrants, in February 2013 Lasith Malinga and Muttiah Muralitharan recorded a video message that was played on Si Lankan television.

"In recent years hundreds of people have lost their lives by making the journey to Australia by sea," said Murali solemnly into the camera. "If you want to travel do it the right way, the safe way. Don't be sorry."

When the refugees arrive at Nauru the facilities are basic, to say the least. The island is a hot, humid place and the camps have no air conditioning; just a few fans that do little more than move hot air around – temperatures get up to 40°C – inside the heavy green canvas tents that each sleep five people.

A nurse who spent three weeks working in the camp at the end of 2012 compared the detention centre to a concentration camp. Marianne Evers, a nurse of more than 40 years' experience, told the Australian media she'd seen suicide attempts, incidences of self-harm, and had heard stories of sexual assault by staff members. While the Australian government denied all this, Amnesty International visited the camp in 2012 and found "a toxic mix of uncertainty, unlawful detention and inhumane conditions creating an increasingly volatile situation on Nauru, with the Australian Government spectacularly failing in its duty of care to asylum seekers."

At the time of writing around 400 men, mostly Sri Lankan, are being held on Nauru. The consensus is that it could be as long as five years before their case is even considered.

Australia points out that they have implemented a few measures to make life more bearable in the camp. There are English classes, the men have access to computer games and the internet. And there is cricket.

There isn't much for the men detained on Nauru to look forward to, but they do have access to some rudimentary cricket equipment. The games go on for hours in a rare and valuable release from the fetid daily monotony of hearing the hot wind thumping against the canvas and the waiting, the interminable, unbearable waiting. When there's cricket to look forward to then life in the camp becomes just that little bit more bearable.

"The Sri Lankans particularly love their cricket," Tara McGuigan, a Salvation Army officer who spent time in the Nauru Topside camp, told the Australian press in 2012. "Some of them are very good."

They may be on a small, worn patch of ground inside a mesh fence next to an abandoned phosphate mine but, when there's a bat or ball in their hand, just for a short while those surroundings can melt away and be replaced by the packed stands of Colombo or Galle, the crashing of the waves dissolving into the roar of the crowd as Jimmy Anderson or Dale Steyn run in and overpitch just by a fraction and are creamed away through the covers to the boundary.

Thanks to cricket, these men – who through sheer desperation have left behind everything they know and risked their lives on an ocean in hope of a better life to end up in a hellish, sweat-soaked tent on a blasted island in the middle of the Pacific with no idea of how long they'll be there – these men can for just a short time every day be Lasith Malinga or Kumar Sangakkara.

If cricket can make life in the Nauru detention camp just that little bit more bearable for these unfortunate men; if looking forward to a game can keep them from thoughts of suicide or the vast, echoing, empty loneliness of their displacement, then cricket is doing its job.

Most of the stories in this book are light-hearted and jolly; cricket as escapism. But cricket in the detention centre on Nauru is a real, potentially life-saving form of escapism.

Nauru, incidentally, was discovered in 1798 by John Fearn, the English captain of the whaling ship *Hunter* on his way from New Zealand to China. He was so taken with it he gave it a name. Pleasant Island.

NEW CALEDONIA

It's 8am on a Saturday morning in September, and two games of traditional cricket are in full swing at Stade de N'Du. From the otherwise empty concrete stand there is a flurry of activity from women wearing brightly coloured, calf-length, loose dresses. Thirteen scattered fielders and four batters make up each game: two to hit, two to run. The umpires are men. There is no protective gear, and bats – flat-faced clubs, really – are one metre long. The bowlers come in off two or three paces. The shots are mostly vigorous leg-side flails. With a loud thud, some middle the heavy, fist-sized ball made from the sap of the banyan; others squirt or balloon it into the off side. If the ball slants down leg, the batter tries to connect by flipping her blade behind her legs – a tricky shot for a quick single, at best (even Eoin Morgan hasn't tried this one). Good hand–eye co-ordination is vital: the ball tends to fall apart, causing dangerously unpredictable bounce. It hurts too. National team player Noel Sinyeue recalls how supporters once discouraged him from attempting a catch for fear of injury. He held on, and became an instant 16-year-old hero. Cricket was imported to these perfect islands in the south-west Pacific in the mid-19th century by British Protestant missionaries, who tried to convert the naturally competitive Melanesians to the sport as a replacement for more violent pastimes. The game rapidly absorbed indigenous rituals, and the number of registered players has since spiralled to 2,600 in 72 clubs. They field several teams for men, women and youngsters, making cricket one of the most popular New Caledonian sports – popular enough to survive Napoleon III's annexation of "Nouvelle-Calédonie" in 1853, and 160 years of enduring French jurisdiction.

The game is so deeply ingrained in the culture that, some years ago, a New Caledonian brewery chose the silhouette of a female cricketer as the logo for its beer, Adele. Sadly, the beer wasn't a success. Neither has been international cricket. Although it has been played in New Caledonia for decades, there is a hard core of only around 30 experienced cricketers. In the 2003 Pacific Games, the men's team suffered one of the heaviest defeats in 50-over cricket, by 468 runs: Papua New Guinea 502 for nine, New Caledonia 34 all out. But the enthusiasts are hopeful that burgeoning partnerships with traditional clubs can help drive New Caledonia to ICC Affiliate status. *Neil Godden*, **Wisden 2013**

There are always extenuating circumstances for a label like this, but poor New Caledonia do have a decent – if that's the right word – claim to being the worst national cricket team in the world. Since playing their first match as a competitive nation in 1979 against the New Hebrides at the South Pacific Games in Fiji, New Caledonia have lost every single game they've played, without exception. No draws, no flukey wins when everything just seems to go right, nothing, just a cycle of loss that may be unparalleled in world cricket history. It's more than 30 years of relentless, unbroken defeat. And they're not only defeats, they're *heavy* defeats. The New Caledonians are handed an absolute walloping every time they pull on a pair of whites in anger.

The 2003 example cited above is not even their biggest shellacking. That came four years later, again at the hands of Papua New Guinea, again at the South Pacific Games. Three Papua New Guineans scored centuries as the poor New Caledonian bowlers were bullied to the tune of 572 for seven from 49 overs (such was the carnage that the umpires lost count of the number of overs bowled. Either that or they felt that the lads from New Caledonia had suffered enough). When New Caledonia were then skittled out for 62, it meant a loss by a colossal 510 runs. That would be humiliating enough in a two-innings game, but in a 50-over match? There can't be many heavier defeats than that in the history of the game at any level. Still, if they could take any consolation from the game, their innings had at least improved on the 20 for which they'd been dismissed by Fiji a few days earlier, having first restricted their opponents to a relatively parsimonious 403 for seven.

Now, having been part of a team that was once bowled out for 10 and for whom the beer match was practically a weekly occurrence, I am in no position nor have I any desire to laugh up my sleeve at this extraordinary sequence of merciless, thumping defeats. On the contrary, I have nothing but admiration and respect for the New Caledonian cricketers. Defining the spirit of cricket is a bit like trying to build a pyramid out of live eels, but whatever it is I'm pretty sure it's right there at the heart of the New Caledonian cricket team.

It can't exactly be fun being ritually humiliated every time you step onto the cricket field. What level of motivation must it take to be a New Caledonian bowler, haring in and giving everything at each delivery in the knowledge that, more often than not, your very best efforts will be thrashed to or over the boundary? Every ball, every over, every match, every season. And still you come back, still you practise in the nets, still you aim to improve every aspect of your game, still you walk out on to the field determined to represent your country to the very best of your ability. And still your efforts are smashed to all parts of the ground even by the late middle order of relative cricketing minnows. It must be that unquenchable flame of hope that burns in all of us, no matter how poor a cricketer we may be. Maybe this time we'll be lucky, maybe this time a few iffy decisions will go our way, maybe this time my yorker will really be a yorker instead of a juicy half-volley, maybe this time the catches will stick, maybe this time my cover-drives will go between the fielders instead of straight to them, maybe this time I'll make some runs. Maybe this is the day we finally win a game; the day we taste for the first time the sweet euphoria of victory.

On the face of it New Caledonia shouldn't have a record as bad as they have. With a population of a quarter of a million there should be a better pool of talent than on many other Pacific islands. They even had a pioneering first-class cricketer: William Nelson Gemmill, born at Thio on New Caledonia, who played 47 times for Glamorgan in the 1920s, including their very first game as a first-class county.

The answer may lie in the fact that most of the cricket played out there is as described above: generally a women's game, in a version adapted from the English as introduced by missionaries in the 19th century similar to *kirikiti* on other islands. The New Caledonian version is played by the indigenous Kanak women, is 13-a-side, there are no wides, the bats are large affairs carved by the local tribal sculptor. and the balls are made from the curdled sap of the banyan tree.

But – colourful, cultural and empowering as that form of cricket may be – I am still drawn to the men's national team like a midge to a barbecue. The whole "it's not about the winning it's about the taking part" thing is a hoary old, faintly patronising cliché, but the way the New Caledonian cricket team keeps on turning up and turning up in the knowledge of inevitable heavy defeat suggests to me that the soul of the game is safe there, even if the windows of cars parked anywhere near a cricket match involving New Caledonia are not.

NIUE ISLAND

The fielder, high in a coconut tree, throws the ball to one of his 39 team-mates at ground level, desperate to prevent his opponent completing the maximum sixth run. The batter, holding the triangular bat, crafted by his forefathers, prepared by an entire family and handed down through the generations, readies himself for the next ball, which may come from any direction, depending on the location of the fielder. The pace is frenetic, thanks to local tip-and-run rules, and the atmosphere vibrant, as the spectators sing traditional songs and applaud good play. The field, located in the

main village square, has no designated boundary, meaning the rubber ball will be fielded in unlikely places, from the top of a coconut tree to some house's washing basket. But amidst the action – and where 80 players might bat in a day – there is still time for moral redemption. A series of ducks or getting out to an unlikely catch is a sign that someone didn't listen to traditional beliefs. Time out is called for a meeting amongst the unlucky team and a confession is sought. The question will be asked: "Did one of you sleep with someone's wife or something?" Play only resumes once the guilty party pays a fine – a different slant on the MCC's "Spirit of Cricket". Niue is a coral island in the Pacific, home to 3,000 people. And cricket, of a kind that would be considered untraditional elsewhere, has a traditional role in Niuan society, and is part of the recovery process for a place battered by Cyclone Heta in January 2004. As the first sport adopted by Niuans, it earned a cultural niche: games involved whole villages, both on and off the field, and the host provided a feast. Nowadays it's b-y-o. This match is the main event of a week-long celebration of the anniversary of Niue attaining self-government, in association with New Zealand, in 1974. It is a tradition associated with certainty. As the island moves forward to an uncertain future, it looks outward – and local officials are seeking kit so they can establish "English" cricket as well.
Tony Munro, **Wisden 2006**

NORFOLK ISLAND

Cricket on Norfolk Island, an Australian outpost in the Western Pacific, looked like dying in the mid 1990s, but has experienced a remarkable revival. The turning point was the Bounty Day match in 1997, which rekindled interest after a four-year break. The fixture dates back at least to 1876: it commemorates (on June 8) the arrival of the *Bounty* mutineers on the island, and is always played between the descendants of the mutineers, who were transferred here from Pitcairn in 1856, and all-comers. There is a re-enactment of the landing, followed by a community picnic within the walls of the ruined convict settlement, and then a friendly match, with many in period costume. By the 1920s, as many as six teams were also playing routine matches, and there were scheduled fixtures against Lord Howe Island, but by 1993 it was impossible to find even 22 cricketers. Now there are three senior and two junior teams, and regular visiting sides from Australia. The ground, Kingston Oval, dates back to 1838; a 160th anniversary match in 1998 had to be postponed following 12 inches of overnight rain. There is very high humidity, and drinks breaks can be long and leisurely. Owing to a lack of qualified umpires, there are no lbw decisions, which creates interesting situations when newcomers appeal for a plumb leg-before. *Haydn Evans and Bob Wellham,* **Wisden 2001**

Cricket on Norfolk Island, 800 miles east of Brisbane in the South Pacific, goes back a long way. The first reference we have is from the diaries of an Ensign Best of the 80th Regiment who arrived on the *James Pattinson* in August 1838 to work at the penal colony for a six-month tour of duty. Best kept a detailed diary of his experiences, in which we find him preparing for a cricket match.

"8th and 9th October: As we proposed opening the cricket season on the 10th with a match between the two regiments I devoted these two days to getting the ground into some sort of order and practising," he wrote. "The ground was in a wretched state cut up by carts and overgrown by weeds. This work, my garden and stockyard, with my bathe in the morning, and evening's read, left me most anxious for bedtime which I make 10 o'clock."

After all that hard work, bathing and reading, match day finally dawned.

"10th: There was great excitement; in the Barracks men rushing violently about and betting figs of tobacco on the result of the game, on the cricket ground a pitching of wickets and tents. At half past 12 the playing commenced and lasted till five when the 50th were declared victorious. This was a result I had expected, few of our men having taken a bat in hand since leaving England ... A pig with a soaped tail was then turned loose and afforded great amusement after which the men ran races in sacks. All these diversions having ceased we returned the men with the pig to their barracks and we to my room where dinner was ready; when this was disposed of we adjourned to the mess room and danced all night ..."

For all the pizzazz and hootenanny that surrounds the IPL, there aren't enough cricket teams celebrating victories by soaping up pigs and letting them run around the place any more. And there certainly aren't enough sack races. Maybe instead of the Super Over ...?

The first reference to the Bounty Day matches appears just over 40 years after Ensign Best and the soapy porcine shenanigans. When Elizabeth Colenso arrived on Norfolk Island in the 1870s she'd not long finished translating both the Old and New Testaments into Maori, a task that took her the best part of 20 years. She also arrived on the back of a divorce from her missionary husband William, whom she'd discovered had fathered a child with Elizabeth's Maori maid. She arrived on Norfolk Island in 1876 and stayed for more than 20 years, teaching and ministering to the island population where even now her memory is regarded with great affection. Not least because it's thanks to Elizabeth Colenso that we have the first reference to Bounty Day cricket.

"On June 11th, 1879, the Norfolkers celebrated the exodus from Pitcairn Island to Norfolk Island by a cricket match which was played on a grassy lawn in front of the old administrative buildings in the town," she wrote. "The descendants of the *Bounty* played the rest, and the *Bounty* eleven was so well dressed-up to represent commodore, captain, etc. that one could imagine that a man-of-war was in. All the Mission personnel were invited, a bountiful dinner being provided."

It's possible that the annual match had begun a few years earlier thanks to the Bishop of Melanesia, John Patterson. Patterson had captained the Second XI at Eton, and when he arrived on Norfolk Island in 1867 to set up a teacher training school, one of his first tasks was to clear a cricket field and teach the boys to play. As most of these lads would go on to missions in the Solomon Islands and all across Micronesia, it's fair to say the Kingston Oval, as the ground became known, played an important part in disseminating cricket around the South Pacific.

The Bounty Day celebrations mark the anniversary of the arrival of 184 Pitcairn Islanders, all descendants of the *Bounty* mutineers, who had outgrown the limited resources on Pitcairn. When Norfolk Island's penal colony closed in 1856 Queen Victoria, impressed by their piety, granted the facilities to the displaced Pitcairners. They arrived on the *Morayshire* on June 8, 1856, seasick after a month at sea and in a torrential downpour. Fortunately the annual celebration in their memory usually goes with a bit more of a swing than their actual arrival. To this day players who share surnames with the original Bounty settlers are a shoo-in for the Bounty XI.

Bishop Patterson must have given the game a pretty solid grounding, as it appears cricket on Norfolk Island has always been played to a reasonably high standard. Take this account by Sir Pelham Warner, who visited Norfolk Island on a tour of the Pacific in 1894.

"A match had been arranged for me, I think, because they had heard that I had been a cricketer, and they wished me to exhibit my prowess. Hard hitters themselves, and judging the value of a hit chiefly by the height and distance that the ball flew, they believed that I should send the ball well over the tall pines that surrounded the ground. They were disappointed, however. The wicket was very rough, and I had scarcely touched a bat for four years. A big islander, John Pantatun ('Hotband'), with a fine high action, sent me down a trimmer for my first ball, and I succumbed. Then I heard, for the first time, an island war-whoop, which staggered me more than the ball which had bowled me."

Warner doesn't record whether any pigs were soaped up to mark the occasion of his dismissal.

NORTHERN CYPRUS

What hope of cricket uniting the Mediterranean's divided island? The game has been played inside British sovereign territories on Cyprus since the Second World War, and spread beyond the barracks by enthusiastic expatriate communities – but only in the south. Among the 300,000 citizens living north of the green line, cricket has barely registered. That is not surprising given that no country in the world except Turkey recognises the Republic of Northern Cyprus. There are no international flights, so foreign visitors arrive from mainland Turkey, or cross from the south. Yet globalisation has brought to the north a sizeable university population, and several hundred Pakistanis who live and work here and are fanatical about cricket. Along with a British expat community of perhaps 12,000 – some of them coaches and umpires – there is a good pot of cricket talent. A short-lived league existed nine years ago, using equipment donated by the UN. And the Pakistanis play avidly in their spare time, usually with a tennis ball on whatever space they can find. But the first properly organised match took place in May 2010, following a friendly wager between Brian Thomas, head of Kyrenia's Royal British Legion branch, and Hussain Zulfiqar, the owner of a Pakistani restaurant. Without official assistance, the organisers managed to procure sponsorship, a stadium from the Pumas rugby team, and cricket gear belonging to another era from the British Army in Dekhelia. The master of ceremonies was 102-year-old Peggy McAlpine, the world's oldest paraglider. Astonishingly, more than 300 people – including a few bemused

Turkish Cypriots – came out to watch this entirely community event, although the British expats were clearly overawed by the gravity of the occasion: they were swiftly dismissed for 35, then dropped four catches as the youthful Pakistani waiters and students swept to an eight-wicket victory. There is a great deal of interest in making the fixture annual, forming teams to play in a regular league, and engaging the local population. A match between teams from north and south might be theoretically possible – if it takes place on British or UN territory. *Brian Thomas*, **Wisden 2011**

NORTH KOREA

Cricket exists even in this isolated country. Matches in Pyongyang are very social occasions, a chance for some of the resident expats to escape the city and head for a nice picnic site that happens to have a suitable patch of land nearby. Although our game is very much improvised, and the exact form often depends on whether there are any locals picnicking nearby, it does involve two sets of stumps and real bats, if not whites. We do, however, have our own Pyongyang Cricket Club shirt. Numbers depend on availability: it can be up to 30. But despite the rapid turnover of expats, we seem to be able to maintain a hardcore of Brits and Aussies to provide instant coaching for the newcomers. Last year some of the keener players moved on to a faster six-a-side game on a football pitch. These included the North Korean groundsman who, it turned out, had in his youth been a professional baseball player in Japan. Once he had worked out that the bowler is supposed to pitch the ball, he did well, even if his action fell outside ICC guidelines. To satisfy local curiosity and build a few bridges with our contacts, we organised a match involving Korean embassy staff, which was a very good social event. When we play, a few Koreans will sometimes stand and watch from a distance, very respectfully. *David Slinn*, **Wisden 2005**

When Matthew Engel launched Cricket Round the World in 1993 he can't possibly have envisaged some of the weird and wonderful places from where copy would arrive. Remote islands, former Soviet states and African nations emerging from war and genocide, for example. One thing's fairly sure, he would never have predicted North Korea ever appearing in the pages of *Wisden*.

Arguably the world's last true pariah state, North Korea does not on the face of it look like a place where you'd ever find a game of cricket. In fact it does not on the face of it look like a place where anyone has even *heard* of cricket. Mass gymnastic displays are more North Korea's thing: why bother with the unpredictability and uncertain outcomes of a duel between bat and ball when you can get 10,000 gymnasts into a stadium performing intricately synchronised choreography and iconography for the viewing pleasure of a chubby man with a hairstyle that appears to have been administered with a food mixer, who happens to run the country?

Football is popular in North Korea, although it's now a long time since Pak Doo Ik and his team-mates emerged from the unknown into the glamorous surroundings of Ayresome Park, Middlesbrough, to beat Italy and give Portugal the fright of their lives before disappearing from both the 1966 World Cup and the global sporting map again. But cricket in North Korea? Even Coca-Cola hasn't infiltrated north of the 38th Parallel since the Korean War, so what hope has a game that is – rightly or wrongly – still seen by many as a symbol of old-fashioned, bayonet-charging, moustache-waxing imperialism?

Inevitably the momentum behind North Korean cricket came from expats, of whom Pyongyang seems to boast a surprisingly high number. There are reports of a Pyongyang Cricket Club existing back in 2002, organised by the head of the European Union aid office in the city. He left for India soon afterwards, but games did apparently continue, with the expats congregating at the Oun Revolutionary Site – where a young Kim Jong-Il underwent his military service – for rudimentary games with rudimentary equipment watched by curious and occasionally suspicious locals.

The reported existence of Pyongyang CC shirts is enough to have collectors of cricketana firing up their salivary glands, although this incarnation of Pyongyang CC seems to have died out by 2008 – which is when North Korea staged its first-ever cricket tournament.

This was a triangular affair comprising two teams emanating from the pioneering Shanghai Cricket Club and a Pyongyang Cricket Club side "specially formed for the occasion". The Shanghai teams – called, with an admirable nod towards diplomacy, Reunification and Juche (the name of Kim-Il Sung's political thesis) – were made up of British, Australian and South African expats. The Pyongyang side included the tourists' two government minders, the coach driver (a Mr Li who, it turned out, had played professional baseball in Japan in his younger days), two lads from the tour company that organised the trip, and the man from DHL, whose company had provided the matting wicket for the tournament.

Visas were secured, permission to stage the tournament was granted from the North Korean sports ministry, and the matting wicket was unfurled with great ceremony at Taesongsan Park, customarily the setting for Pyongyang's May Day festivities and the only piece of land in the city suitable for a cricket match.

The pitch was in the shadow of the Tsaesongsan Fortress, a large and impressive pagoda-style structure dating back to the third century and lovingly reconstructed after being badly damaged by American bombs during the Korean War. As pavilions go, it was a beauty.

More than 800 runs were scored in the three Twenty20 matches that saw Juche emerge victorious to lift the first Pyongyang Friendship Cup. The Koreans involved took to the game reassuringly well and played a big part in the success of the event. Some cricket traditions were observed – cucumber sandwiches were served at tea – while some innovative new ones were introduced, such as the tea interval being accompanied by a Korean accordion band.

It seems the Pyongyang Friendship Cup is still in Shanghai, as there doesn't appear to have been a repeat of the tournament. While cricket news out of Pyongyang is hard to come by, who knows, maybe the local involvement in the Cup meant that Pyongyang CC is still going strong in some form. Maybe one day the North Korean leader himself may take up the game. Let's not forget that Kim Jong-Un's father Kim Jong-Il apparently scored 11 holes in one the first time he ever picked up a golf club, going round 34 under par in his first-ever 18 holes in 1994. If Kim Jong-Un happened to wander down to Tsaesongsan Park – I don't know, maybe to have a look at the gate or something – and found a game in progress, he would doubtless caress his way to a flawless quadruple-century in 40 minutes then bowl out the opposition with a triple hat-trick and a direct-hit run-out thrown from behind the Tsaesongsan Fortress while facing backwards and conducting the accordion band with his other hand.

NORWAY

Cricket survives and thrives in Norway, despite the problems caused by the very harsh winters. Football as well as cricket is a summer sport, and so there is a shortage of available playing space. It took a long while to persuade the authorities that a patch of grass was not quite enough. The big breakthrough came in 1996 when, after a lot of hard work and persuasion, the Oslo Sports Council agreed to provide an artificial pitch and two practice wickets. The climate has caused some teething problems, but these will be overcome. Already, the better facilities have helped standards, and in 1998 nine teams will compete for the league title. Most of the players are migrants from Asia, and one of the teams is Sri Lankan. When they play, the whole family attends, and local residents have been intrigued to see a crowd of 200 watching cricket at 10am on a Sunday. *Bob Gibb*, **Wisden 1998**

OMAN

Oman's capital can claim the title of the driest city in the cricket-playing world, traditionally leading to rough and unsafe surfaces. So perhaps it is no surprise that the country's best-known Arab cricketer, HH Qais bin Khalid Al Said, a cousin of the Sultan, learned the game at Millfield School rather than Muscat. But now Al Emerat, the first fully turf ground in the Sultanate, has been assiduously prepared for the new season. For the first time, fielders will be able to attack the ball, rather than edge in tentatively from the boundary trying to predict bounce and trajectory on scorched-earth ground. Batsmen and bowlers will finally get off matting wickets, and learn to deal with spin and seam. When Oman finished 15th out of 16 at the 2012 World Twenty20 qualifying tournament, the sports ministry expressed their "deep disappointment", and enquired why more Omani nationals had not been considered for selection. As in many Gulf states, league matches are often subcontinental corporate affairs between expat semi-professionals – with a single token Omani thrown in to satisfy league membership regulations. Yet Oman has the best record in the Middle East for producing indigenous cricketers: around 200 of the 1,100 regular players in the country are Arabs. Oman is the only country in the region to insist upon three nationals in their representative youth sides from 16 upwards. And, as coaches head into schools, more and more Arab boys and girls are discovering, to their surprise, that this peculiar game is their nation's most successful international sport. *Paul Bird*, **Wisden 2013**

PANAMA

In 2000 Panama fielded a combined team – irrespective of religious ties – for what is believed to be the first time in 36 years. A national side played two fixtures against a touring Venezuelan XI, winning the first game and gaining the edge in the second before rain intervened. In the opening game, Asif Patel scored 34 of his 38 in one over. Unfortunately we have no cricket grounds so the game has to be played in football or baseball stadiums. Cricket in Panama dates back to about 1900, when West Indians arrived to help build the Panama Canal. Cricket then faded away until the Asian community began to establish itself. Religious conflicts meant that separate tournaments for Muslims and Hindus evolved. Games continue to be controversial: last season during their semi-final in the Muslim competition, Bhatan CC walked off the field in protest against time-wasting by Paraiso CC, who were due to win on run-rate if the game was not completed by six o'clock. *Saleh and Musaji Banah*, **Wisden 2001**

PERU

The Lima Cricket and Football Club has now completed 15 years' play without losing a single minute to rain (which is a good reason to visit for our annual Easter tournament). We play from February to April, and our pitch is pretty rough because football is played in winter. It is a grass surface but a broadleaf grass which forms a mat under the leaves. It is not conducive to driving, and many a fine innings has been played without a single cover-drive, but plenty of lusty blows over the boundary. We now have a hard core of 25 players (plus tourists, who are welcome), more than at any time in my 15 years here. There has not been an influx, but the Brits at the cricket club have now joined forces with local Asians. When I had been here a year or two and was driving past the clifftop park in Lima, I saw a couple of what I assumed were locals playing tip and run with a cricket bat. Good God, I thought, dived out of the car and talked to them. Of course, they turned out to be Indians, and were immediately invited along. We now have a regular hotly contested fixture: India and Pakistan v Rest of the World, whose team includes our one Peruvian, Jorge Pancorvo, an excellent wicketkeeper (aged 51 but still fit). *Vivian Ash*, **Wisden 2005**

RUSSIA

In July, an English touring team, the Explorers, played what was reported to be the first formal match in Moscow since the Bolshevik Revolution. Their opponents were the MCC: the newly-formed Moscow Cricket Club. Owing to a misunderstanding, the pitch was originally laid out for a croquet match. Broom-handles had to be used in place of stumps: the man bringing some of the kit was stopped at Heathrow because he had forgotten to get a visa.
Wisden 1994

It may have been the first match in Moscow since the Revolution but the Explorers' game continued a fine Russian tradition of cricket 'misunderstandings'. According to F.S. Ashley-Cooper's wonderful 1927 book *Cricket Highways and Byways*, in Imperial times St Petersburg boasted two clubs – remarkable enough in such a cricket outpost but even more so when you consider how the first set of laws translated into Russian had the length of the pitch at 12ft and insisted that no fielder was allowed within 40ft of the batsman.

When I tracked down one of the Explorers, Mark Rice-Oxley, he confessed that "I can't quite remember what happened," but when pressed recalled that there was cake, tea and a string quartet at the tea interval, that the game was played just off Komsomolsky

Prospekt on the southern side of Moscow "in the lee of one of the Stalin wedding-cake buildings", that it was "the weekend the Central Bank arbitrarily declared a currency reform that would make old roubles worthless, so many of us were thinking of that rather than the cricket" – and most importantly that "I was out for one, but did get a hatful of wickets on a track more spiteful than Stalin in his heyday."

The Moscow side – largely comprised of expats but with at least one Russian and one native of Belarus – scored a semi-respectable 112 but, mainly thanks to an impressive 45 from Richard Atkinson, the Explorers emerged from a tight game victorious.

The Explorers were continuing a noble touring tradition: as far back as 1865 a *Handbook for Travellers in Russia, Poland and Finland* was advising that "in summer the tourist can join the matches of the St Petersburg cricket club". The sporting visitor could also, next to the cricket ground, "shoot blackcock, capercailzie, snipe and duck", which are birds, presumably, rather than the names of the St Petersburg bowling attack.

At least three Russian Tsars had exposure to cricket: in 1814 "upon the glorious termination of the war in Belgium", Alexander I joined George III and the magnificently named Prussian Marshal Gebhardt Leberecht von Blucher in watching Eton schoolboys playing at Frogmore on the outskirts of Windsor. Alexander's son Nicholas I saw a cricket match when visiting the English naval dockyard at Chatham, apparently remarking, "I don't wonder at the courage of you English, when you teach your children to play with cannon-balls." Nicholas would go on to charge headlong into war with the Ottoman Empire in 1853, believing that he had British diplomatic support. He didn't. In fact, Britain would side with the Ottomans in what became the Crimean War. Could his belief that as long as the hard-as-nails Brits had his back everything would be all right have stemmed at least in part from watching a bunch of jolly jack tars knocking a cricket ball around Chatham?

This Russian belief that cricketers were made of tough stuff surfaced again in 1875 when the crew of the British royal yacht *Osborne* played a match in the dockyard at St Petersburg. As Ashley-Cooper recounts, "a message arrived from the chef de police demanding an explanation of the presence of this 'force of warriors' in the midst of the Russian Woolwich."

Finally, completing a hat-trick of Tsars, the ill-fated Nicholas II was apparently enough of a cricket fan to lay a pitch at his Peterhof palace. But this would be the last Russian cricket action until the Iron Curtain had clanged shut, reopened and the Explorers arrived in Moscow while the string quartet tuned up.

In 2008 Sir Tim Rice's Heartaches team, featuring Allan Lamb, travelled to St Petersburg and played an "England" side made up of diplomats and expats in the Mayakovsky Garden in the sumptuous grounds of the State Russian Museum.

These days, however, Russian cricket is not just the preserve of the expat, the visiting sailor or even celebrity librettist: in 2012 Cricket Russia staged its first open cricket academy in Moscow, and 100 Russian children and 30 Russian adults turned out. The pitches were, presumably, more than 12ft long.

RWANDA

They say sport and politics don't mix, but Rwanda's increasingly strong, not to say unlikely, ties with cricket sit comfortably with the efforts of the country's president, Paul Kagame, to sever links with its former colonial masters in France and Belgium and cosy up to the Commonwealth. Kagame, who learned the game while a refugee in neighbouring Uganda, still blames the French for the massacre of around one million Tutsis in 1994, and is only too happy to see young men in this Francophone nation speaking English on the field of play. It is poignant that the country's only cricket ground, the Kicukiro Oval, lies next to the École Technique, where almost

3,000 Tutsis were slaughtered by members of the Hutu tribe that year. "When we first started playing, we found piles of bones on the boundary over there," Julius Mbaraga, the captain of the Right Guards, Rwanda's first cricket club, told *The Times*. The newspaper claimed one game at the ramshackle venue was interrupted after an unexploded landmine was found at silly mid-on. Cricket was first introduced to the country in 2000 by returning Tutsi boys who had learned the game in exile. The locals' enthusiasm – Rwanda has five teams – persuaded the British charity Cricket Without Boundaries to organise a six-day clinic for coaches in November, while the Conservative Party have donated six bags of kit and equipment.
Wisden 2008

Cricket Round the World has brought us many stories of the game taking hold in unlikely places, but few tales are as poignant as that of the game in Rwanda. This is no story of jolly expats encouraging locals to join in their curious game; rather this is an organic, indigenous growth of a sport; a growth born out of tragedy and exile.

There was no cricket culture to speak of in Rwanda before the 1994 genocide when the Hutus set out to obliterate the Tutsis. Those who escaped the slaughter by fleeing into Kenya, Tanzania and Uganda experienced cricket for the first time and, when it was safe for them to return, the game came home with them.

Traumatised by one of the most vicious and bloody eruptions of ethnic hatred in history, not to mention being one of the world's poorest nations, Rwanda, blighted, blood-soaked Rwanda, was about as far removed from the gentle well-to-do culture of cricket as it was possible to be. Yet the game has not only taken hold in the country since the genocide: it has flourished. The Rwanda Cricket Association was formed in 1999, ICC Affiliate status was granted the following year, and in 2002 the game forged in foreign refugee camps found a semi-permanent home at one of the most notorious locations in the country.

In 1994 the École Technique Officielle in the Kigali suburb of Kicugiro was Rwanda's only technical college. It also became a safe haven for some of those threatened by the mass killings, defended by UN peacekeeping troops from Belgium. However, when ten UN peacekeepers were killed elsewhere in the capital the Belgians moved out, leaving the 5,000 or so Tutsis gathered at the college entirely at the mercy of the Hutus. Mercy was, however, in short supply. Estimates of the numbers killed in the ensuing slaughter vary; 2,500 appears to be the most conservative figure accepted as roughly accurate as the college became one of the most notorious killing grounds of the entire genocide.

Eight years later the college became the home of Rwandan cricket. The serene, gentle rhythms of the game were a long way from the horrors of 1994, yet for a sport that began as part of a healing process among the displaced and dispossessed to be played on such a notorious piece of ground became almost a symbol the nation's nascent emergence from its collective trauma.

Today cricket development continues apace. Under the auspices of the Rwandan Cricket Stadium Foundation work is underway on a permanent, purpose-built home for Rwandan cricket in the capital Kigali. Thanks to the tireless fund-raising and coaching work of Englishman Oli Broom, who headed the foundation (and whose ability and willingness to go the extra mile knows no bounds: in 2013 he ran up a mountain to raise money for corrective dental work for a Rwandan cricketer who'd had his teeth knocked out by a ball that lifted off a length) the new ground is planned to be ready in time for the 20th anniversary of the 1994 massacre.

With a new ground, an estimated 60 per cent of the population aged under 20 and climatic conditions making cricket possible almost all year round, the game in Rwanda has a brighter future than almost anywhere in the world.

Few countries would take being described as "the next Afghanistan" as any kind of compliment, but in terms of cricket developing at an extraordinary rate of progress having emerged from incomprehensible horrors it's a compliment that suits Rwanda perfectly.

ST HELENA

The cricket season on St Helena (population: 5,500) runs from January to July. Eight teams play one-day matches of two innings a side on a matting pitch at Francis Plain, where in 1886 a fielder is alleged to have died chasing a ball over a cliff; a repetition is still theoretically possible. After many years of ascendancy by Jamestown B, Western B won the 1994 championship ahead of Levelwood A, who won the knockout. Jamestown B, however, provided two individual highlights: left-arm spinner Eric George, the chairman of the cricket association who is in his sixties, took eight for 39 before announcing his retirement at the end of the season; his son Gavin averaged 71 with the bat. Play traditionally continues in the rain, but two matches had to be postponed in 1994 because the Royal Mail ship, the only link with the outside world, was in port for its bi-monthly visit. *Fraser M. Simm*, **Wisden 1995**

SEYCHELLES

Cricket in Seychelles is in a somewhat parlous state. The Seychelles Cricket Association is laughingly referred to as the Sri Lankan Cricket Association as without their expatriates there would be no cricket here. For eight years I have been taking the young players to practice, but the locals kick a football around and across the wicket, disrupting the cricket so much that many are scared to attend. Still, five teams are playing. We are obliged to play with a mat on a football field, which is positively lethal; everybody now wears a helmet when batting. Our reciprocal matches with Mauritius have been rather one-sided in their favour. We have support from our National Sports Council, but they are obliged to give priority to sports which are enjoyed by the Seychellois, which is unlikely ever to include cricket. *Anthony Coster,* **Wisden 1998**

SLOVENIA

One of the least-known and prettiest parts of Europe has begun playing cricket. Slovenia – the peaceful and prosperous end of what was once Yugoslavia – acquired a team when the Royal Hague Cricket Club of Holland were looking for fixtures. Even though cricket had never been played there, a motley crew of expatriates and one brave Slovene rose to the challenge. We cheekily asked the president of Slovenia, Milan Kucan, if we could use his name. He not only agreed but attended the match, and I explained to him the origin of various cricketing phrases. "Oh," he replied, "so you might say the American attitude to our application to join NATO is not quite cricket." The game was the lead sports item on national TV and led to a fixture in Austria. The next challenge is to find our own ground near Ljubljana. *Francis King,* **Wisden 1999**

To say that cricket had never been played in Slovenia before 1998 isn't quite true. Cricket was actually introduced to the former Yugoslav republic long before independence, as far back as the 1970s in fact. Indeed, the roots of Slovene cricket lie in the unlikely surroundings of Birchington-on-Sea on the north-eastern coast of Kent. Previously best-known for seeing off the artist and poet Dante

Gabriel Rossetti, who died there in 1882 having arrived planning to improve his health, it's possible the town may grow to become a cricket shrine for Slovenians. For it was in a back garden in Birchington-on-Sea that the Slovene game was born.

It was 1974 when a 13-year-old named Borut Čegovnik left Yugoslavia for the first time to study English. Staying in Birchington-on-Sea with the family of his English pen-pal – whose father, Charles Nash, played for the local club – Borut was introduced to the game through a combination of watching his host play and long coaching sessions in the back garden with his epistolary chum. The young visitor fell in love with the game, and returned to Slovenia with his luggage increased to the tune of a bat, ball and set of stumps. Back home in the old mining town of Mežica, close to the border with Austria, Borut introduced the game to his friends, they formed the Mežica Cricket Club which still flourishes today and, when he later moved to the capital Ljubljana, Borut took the game with him.

Today Dr Borut Čegovnik is a leading cardiologist and the president of the Slovenian Cricket Association. Slovenia is an Affiliate Member of the ICC, boasts nine cricket clubs, and has a national team that's more than holding its own in European competitions. All thanks to a summer language exchange and a bit of healthy exercise. Despite the unexpectedly cricket-heavy theme of his 1974 trip to north Kent, it's not believed Dr Čegovnik's English studies suffered unduly.

SOUTH KOREA

Cricket revived in Korea in the late 1980s through the expatriate Indian community. It is played by six teams of nine-a-side (representing Australia, India, New Zealand, British Embassy, International All Stars and the Rest of the World) over 15 overs on a small irregular-shaped soccer field controlled by the US Military in the UN Compound. We bowl only from one end, on a wicket that consists of bare ground, covered by one layer of rubberised matting overlaid by felt carpet; despite the small ground, bowlers tend to have the upper hand – shooters and fliers are par for the course. The scoring rules are modified but complex, taking into account the back wall (four if hit on the full), the willow tree (six) and the embankment with the blackberries. The regular competition is played twice a year, spring and autumn. India were the winners in spring 1994. In the autumn, the New Zealanders arranged for the former Test player, Rod Latham, to turn up as a casual late inclusion. The game was washed out, even though the Kiwis were still keen to play in half an inch of mud. Anyone wandering through Korea is welcome to view this grand spectacle on Sunday afternoons. *John A. Kaminsky*, **Wisden 1995**

SPAIN

Spanish cricket continues to be dogged by lack of funds, with the Asociacion Espanola de Cricket supported by a few good men and true. This situation mainly affects the senior clubs, whose funds do not stretch to the luxury of travelling between six and ten hours to compete in league games at a cost of anything up to £2,000 per game. Sporting Alfas CC beat Javea CC in this year's cup final. Training sessions in both Kwik Cricket and the hard-ball game are now held several times a week in the Costa Blanca area, with youngsters from the ages of six upward, while a number of Spanish teachers in and around Javea are introducing the game into their curricula. Cricket still remains a mystery for most Spaniards, however: a colleague arrived home looking dishevelled and muddy. And when his Spanish neighbour asked if he had had an accident, he replied: "No, I've only been playing cricket. I'm fine." "And your horse? Is your horse all right?" *Ken Sainsbury*, **Wisden 2000**

SUDAN

As cricket's remote outposts go, Sudan's is one of the remotest. Although the country has several of the prerequisites for a thriving cricket culture – year-round sunshine and historical ties with Britain – the sport has never really caught on with the locals, leaving it largely in the hands of the expats. Friendlies are played between the British Embassy, students at the Khartoum International Community School and their parents, and the DAL Group, a local conglomerate, allowing a variety of Anglo-Saxons, Australasians, Canadians and others to play for the 20 or so overs that seem sensible in the unforgiving heat. Several groups from the subcontinent also play improvised matches on the uneven ground of outer Omdurman, while the presence of Indian, Pakistani and Bangladeshi battalions in the United Nations Mission here has taken social matches to such unlikely places as Juba and Kadugli. But the result of the referendum in January 2011, when the overwhelming majority of Southern Sudan voted for independence, could yet prove significant. If the newly independent south follows in the footsteps of Rwanda by applying for membership of the Commonwealth and the East African Community, what better way to show its bona fides than by establishing the roots of a cricketing culture? Since the region's most famous sportsman, basketball player Luol Deng, typifies the height and build of his people, it is tempting to conclude that any fast-bowling attack could prove quite a lively proposition. *Tony Brennan*, **Wisden 2011**

SURINAM

Cricket, or something resembling it, was first played in Surinam in 1880 when it was Dutch Guiana. In all probability, these first cricketers were indentured Indians. The game became organised with the establishment of Royal Scott's CC in 1885, and a national association, which today is an associate member of the West Indies board, was founded in 1931. As games were played more regularly against sides from neighbouring Guyana (British Guiana) and other West Indian countries, cricket youth teams of the 1980s went on to play for the Dutch national side. Today there are some 25 senior clubs, and the Surinamese Cricket Association have applied for membership of the Cricket Council of the Americas and for Affiliate Membership of the ICC. *Ram Hiralal*, **Wisden 2002**

TAJIKISTAN

In 1997, at the end of Tajikistan's messy five-year civil war that followed the break-up of the Soviet Union, Indian students and exiled Afghans began playing tennis-ball cricket in the capital, Dushanbe. Locals noticed the similarities with *suzi musi*, a traditional Tajik bat-and-ball game, and joined in. There are now eight men's and two women's teams affiliated to the Tajikistan Cricket Federation, and a Pakistani tape-ball community pining for entry. The hotbed is Shahrinaw, 50km west of Dushanbe, where cricket is played at municipality grounds and an orphanage. The TCF will have to hurdle several obstacles to expand cricket in Central Asia's poorest country: internet use is rare, with access to social networking sites cut off at the whim of the government. And around a million Tajik men are drawn to Russia every year for work, in order to feed their families and prop up their country's fragile economy. So it may be women that do the heavy lifting. Assadullah Khan, a former Afghanistan player now coaching in Tajikistan, has declared that, in two years, his all-Tajik women's team will be the best in Asia. In July, Tajikistan played Afghanistan in a three-match series in Shahrinaw – the first women's international games in each country's history. The Afghan team made the journey north across the border with the sponsorship of a private NGO, as women's sport was considered too sensitive an issue for Kabul. The Afghans, clad in headscarves, won 2–1. *James Coyne*, **Wisden 2013**

TRISTAN DA CUNHA

News travels slowly from this South Atlantic island, but the first match for ten years took place there in January 1995 through the initiative of a local official, Alan Waters. The coir matting once used as a surface had long since disappeared, and it was not safe to play with a cricket ball on the concrete, so a rounders ball was used. Some of the older islanders could still handle a bat but were no longer sufficiently co-ordinated to take catches. However, with 60 children among the 300 islanders, Waters saw his chance and ordered a Kwik Cricket set from England. He was also hoping to arrange matches against passing ships, but the cost of adult equipment is prohibitive. British missionaries originally helped the game thrive: among the Victorian pioneers was Edwin Dodgson, Lewis Carroll's brother. The game was also played regularly in the 1950s when the matting was laid at a spot called Hottentot Fence, but that era ended with the volcanic eruption of 1961 which forced the island to be evacuated. *Peter S. Hargreaves*, **Wisden 1997**

TURKEY

The Turkish museum on the Gallipoli peninsula that commemorates the 1915 campaign contains an ageing photograph entitled Kricket Oynuyor. Anzac forces are shown playing cricket on Shell Green, a modest, flat basin secured at a cost of many lives. Despite the "ground" being overlooked by Turkish guns – hence the name – those shown in the photograph appear to be playing with typical vigour. On Anzac Day 1998 (April 25), there was a dawn service at 5am, the time the original landings took place. A commemorative match was then arranged for Shell Green between the Anzacs and the Rest of the World. Hundreds of young Australians and New Zealanders sought to play for the Anzac team. The Rest of the World was more difficult to finalise, and it is not known whether it was to include any Turks. Sadly the heavens opened and the match was abandoned before a ball could be bowled. *Anthony Bradbury,* **Wisden 1998**

UGANDA

Uganda is unique in African cricket: it is the only country where the game is played mainly by the African community. When the country was enduring its national nightmare of tyranny and civil war in the 1970s and early 1980s, and nearly all Asians and Europeans left the country, a small group of enthusiasts kept the game alive in near-impossible circumstances. Under the Amin regime, cricket was regarded as elitist, and the team was often denied permission to play abroad. Once, the square used by the national team was churned up by being used for the start and finish of a motor rally – at the insistence of the sports minister. Now with the country reviving Ugandan cricket is reviving too. In 1997 Uganda won the annual quadrangular tournament against the other countries affiliated to ICC as East and Central Africa (Malawi, Tanzania and Zambia) for only the second time in three decades. In 1998 Uganda hope to break away from this group and achieve Associate Membership of ICC in their own right. Playing standards are not a match for neighbouring Kenya, but the Ugandans' tour of England in 1995, when they won ten games out of 12 against strong club sides, suggests that the team could be a force in future ICC Trophies. **Wisden 1998**

UKRAINE

Cricket is putting down roots in Europe's largest country thanks to the efforts of the Pakistani-born businessman Mohammad Zahoor. The enigmatic Mr Zahoor's calm smile and few words belie a business acumen that helped him survive Ukraine's cut-throat 1990s to rank in 2010 as one of the country's richest men, emerging from the steel industry with an estimated fortune of $1bn. Now he is dedicating himself to a number of pet projects, including the *Kyiv Post* newspaper, the career of his wife, Ukrainian pop diva Kamaliya … and cricket. Zahoor wants Ukraine to send a cricket team to the 2020 Olympics, but has no illusions about the size of the task: current estimates suggest there are no more than 800 players in this country of 42 million. And the village-green tournaments Zahoor has hosted in Kyiv reveal that almost all of them hail from the subcontinent, with less than a handful of Ukrainian-born players. But the Asian presence could serve as an antidote to Ukraine's endemic corruption. John Illingworth, meanwhile, nephew of former England captain Ray, has settled here and captains Kyiv Cricket Club. Another colourful local fan is Sean Carr – son-in-law of former prime minister Yulia Tymoshenko, Ukraine's famous blonde-and-braided Iron Lady. Carr, a tattooed and leathered English biker – when he is not racing his Harley-Davidson across Ukraine's wide steppes – often attends Zahoor's events. *Graham Stack*, **Wisden 2011**

UNITED STATES

Cricket is now being played on a huge scale from New England to California, but the organisation remains far behind the potential. Yet again the USA Cricket Association came under attack for failing to foster the game's development, and there were no obvious

signs of the problem being addressed. Cricket gained some publicity when community leader Ted Hayes and a British insurance broker, David Sentance, helped form a team called LA Kricketts from a group of homeless Los Angeles dropouts. The team toured Britain and played at Hambledon. But this was an exception to the general failure to make the most of the game's possibilities. The feeling is that this may change only if the US qualify for the next World Cup.
Wisden 1996

The story of the LA Kricketts is one of the most extraordinary, uplifting and inspiring ever to appear in Cricket Round the World. Founded in 1995 at the Dome Village Homeless Community by community worker Ted Hayes and British film producer Katy Haber, the Kricketts' philosophy was – and is – to promote sportsmanship, etiquette and fair play, to develop a respect for authority, and foster self-esteem and self-discipline in the midst of the bullet-riddled gang culture of south-central Los Angeles. As Hayes himself put it, "the aim of playing cricket is to teach people how to respect themselves and respect authority so they stop killing each other".

Now known as the Compton Cricket Club, the team plays at the Leo Magnus Cricket Complex in the Van Nuys district, named after the team's former coach Leo "Jingles" Magnus.

On their three tours of Britain subsequent to this entry, in 1997, 1999 and 2001, the Compton players have rapped for Prince Edward, played the Aboriginal All-Stars – the first Aboriginal touring side since 1868 – at Hambledon, presented Gerry Adams with a cricket bat and David Trimble with a hurley, and welcomed Brian Lara into their side for a match against Lashings CC in 2001.

For once the cricket is pretty much secondary to what's being achieved on a wider, deeper level.

"We caught the boys from Compton at that stage in every adolescence where they shift from tagging into full-scale gang activity," says Hayes. It's working too. Former gang member Sergio Pinares has been with the club for 14 years, and told the *Los Angeles Times*, "I guess you could say I switched my gun for a bat. I mean, what would I be doing with my time if I wasn't playing cricket? I would probably have ended up in jail. It's hard to explain, but I love the way everyone carries themselves in cricket. For a person like me, who'd never seen people behave that way, it was special."

The combination of kids from some of the toughest streets in the world who've seen – and in some cases done – some terrible things and the genteel game of cricket is an idiosyncratic one. It really shouldn't work: if you pitched it as a screenplay you'd be laughed out of the room. But it really *does* work, and the Compton Cricket Club is fast approaching two decades of amazing work that shows no sign of slowing any time soon, let alone stopping. Cricket is proving to be the unlikeliest of social saviours in the unlikeliest of settings.

"If the British did anything right," says Ted Hayes, "they did right when they invented cricket."

VENEZUELA

With no domestic tournament and just one ground, at the Caracas Sports Club, Venezuela's cricketers look to visiting teams to give their games some spice. They are not short of cricket, just variety: after all, they play every other week throughout the year. Tourist Sports Club of Miami and a side from Queen's Park Oval, Port-of-Spain, made appearances in 2001 – the latter as part of Trinidad's Independence Day celebrations – and both were expected to return in January 2002 to celebrate the Caracas club's 50th anniversary. Other opponents included teams from Belize, Colombia and Panama. In December 2000, Venezuela competed in the South American Championship in Buenos Aires. All three games, although close, were lost, partly because several leading Venezuelan players could not afford to travel. For the game against eventual winners Argentina A, Venezuela were loaned three boys aged 10, 12 and 14. *Basil Mathura*, **Wisden 2002**

VIETNAM

The Sri Lankan Nalliah Sallathurai was reported to have become the first batsman to score a century in the Vietnamese capital, Hanoi, making 106 for an Indian subcontinent team against an Australian-English side on a matting pitch. **Wisden 1995**

WESTERN SAMOA

Local players in Apia, the capital of Western Samoa, challenged European players to a two-match series involving both the versions of cricket played here: Samoan *kirikiti*, with four-foot bats and a flexible number of players, and the more familiar game. The scoring needed to be audited, but pride was salvaged by both sides in their own codes. "English cricket" here continued through another retrenched year; the senior competition has been reduced from 14 teams to a group of just 30–50 regulars. There are hopes of a revival, stimulated by Samoan men returning from Australasian cities, and the recent arrival of TV from New Zealand. The cost of equipment is a major constraint, and there is a desperate need for visiting teams. The game, however, has survived the ravages of "wild women" – the local name for cyclones. Last time the island was hit, the ground was used as a relief base and taken over by helicopters and roofing iron.

Bob Barlow, **Wisden 1996**